PARABLES OF THE MASTER

A Discussion Guide for Teens

LOUIS O. CALDWELL

Contemporary
Discussion Series

Baker Book House
Grand Rapids, Michigan 49506

Standard Book Number: 8010-2318-1

Copyright © 1964 by Baker Book House Company

Printed in the United States of America
by Dickinson Brothers, Inc., Grand Rapids, Michigan

Formerly published under the title, *He Speaks to YOUth*

Scripture quotations other than those from the King James
Version are taken from *The New Testament in Modern
English* by J. B. Phillips, Copyright © 1958 by J. B.
Phillips, used by permission of The Macmillan Company;
also *The New English Bible* Copyright © The Delegates
of the Oxford University Press and the Syndics of the
Cambridge University Press, 1961, reprinted by permission.

This book is affectionately dedicated to
My sister
Mrs. Joseph (Sally) Clark
and
My brother
Mr. Edgar B. Caldwell

Preface

Jesus is the Great Teacher. His Plan is clear yet direct; His Method is simple yet profound. Man in his effort to devise a guide for living has not been able to approach the Everlasting Truths revealed in the Parables. To relate these Messages to the needs of today's youth is the "heart" of Dr. Caldwell's fascinating book.

Lessons for living are being taught at home, in school, and in church. Because of age and experience adults in every period of history justify leading the young by use of suggestions, directions, and forces believed to be helpful in building productive lives. Youth face problems, experience success and failure, and are emotionally pressed in growing toward their own maturity — pondering what to do, trying to make decisions, and striving for happiness and fulfillment. The blueprint for a useful, worthwhile, and joyous life is the precious treasure buried in God's Word. Adults and youth can work together to uncover wisdom and inspiration for the fruitful use of time, talent, and energy. If we but read the Words of the Master as He taught people who lived and breathed like ourselves, we can see the solutions to the perplexing problems that confuse and torment us in the explosive time in which we live. The wonderful knowledge to be gained is that Jesus has explained what to do, has given examples for decisions, and has provided the Way for complete happiness and total fulfillment.

As young people seek to understand the meaning of the Message of the Scriptures, they are indeed fortunate to have in their hands the words which flow easily through Dr. Caldwell's pages. This inspired guide is geared for the teen mind; those who follow the ideas and suggestions presented will find peace of mind and achievement of God's Plan. The teen space of the total life span may be beautiful and dynamic if Dr. Caldwell's realistic and spiritual interpretations become the motivational strength of the individual.

Dr. LaVerne Carmical
College of Education
University of Houston
Houston, Texas

Contents

How to Sharpen Your Reading Pleasure

Try the following suggestions for profitable reading and see if they'll work for you:

1. CONCENTRATION. Give your best attention to the reading of every parable preceding each chapter. In connection with "being all there," a great English professor had this to say:

> There is one thing we can do, and the happiest people are those who do it to the limit of their ability.

> We can be completely present. We can be all there. We can control the tendency of our minds to wander. . . . It is hard to do this; but it is harder to understand afterward wherein it was we fell so short. It was where and when we ceased to give our entire attention to the person, the opportunity before us.

2. PARTICIPATION. You can enjoy a rich mental participation in reading the parables by asking yourself the following questions: "Why was this parable spoken?" "Which one of the people in the story represents me?" "What is the parable's main idea?" Get involved in the questions, the plot, the people, the purpose, and the point and the parables will come alive.

3. APPLICATION. After you learn the parable, *live* it by putting its lesson into practice at your first opportunity.

If you have never examined the parables of Christ, you will find yourself inspired, surprised, directed, maybe provoked — even enraged. But you will find them more stimulating than the most exciting novel in your school library. In the parables you will discover that Jesus is actually speaking to *you* with fresh meaning, divine understanding, and abiding love.

Bible scholars have found that the parables take up a third of the four gospels: Matthew, Mark, Luke, and John. You won't find all the parables in this book.* However, I hope that what you read will whet your appetite for more.

---

*Bible scholars disagree on the number of parables that Jesus spoke. Estimates vary from 27 to more than 75. The reason for the difference in opinion is found in the way in which scholars define *parable*. If the parable is understood to be a comparison then the number generally accepted is about 30. Those who classify metaphors and proverbial sayings as parables will, of course, find more than 30. An example of the metaphor is found in Matt. 5:13, an example of the proverb in Luke 4:23. This book includes no parables classified as metaphorical or proverbial.

"Nothing Could Have Kept Them Away!"

Teen-agers have a genius for giving life to things, especially words. No other age can match them when it comes to affecting the English language. Teen talk overflows with colorful — and often mystical — expressions, some of which Webster has yet to define!

A survey of America's youth turned up some examples of their lingo, called *Youthese*. Listed below are a few examples:

Youthese	*English Translation*
"Up tight"	"Under tension"
"Out of sight"	"Too great to describe"
"Split"	"Leave a group"
"Cop out"	"Disassociate yourself from something"

Some expressions resisting any kind of meaningful translation are:

> "Kinda like never."
> "Who took the astronaut's crayons?"

Working with teen-agers in many kinds of activities, I sometimes catch such spicy conversational expressions as,

> "A pop test as unexpected as a sonic boom."

11

However, no one has ever given life to language as did the young man Jesus who lived in Palestine almost twenty centuries ago. Everything He saw on earth reminded Him of something He'd left in Heaven. He would share these exciting comparisons with everyone who wanted to hear them. We call His comparisons *parables*, popularly defined as "earthly illustrations of heavenly truths."

Christ crammed His parables so full of youthful zest and timeless truth, that upon hearing Him speak, the people dared to make this great declaration: "Never man spake like this man." The years have not taken away their talent for fascinating new generations. Edwin Markham, the great Christian poet, said of the parables of Jesus, "Of all the world's religious literature, these are its crowning glory."

He must have made quite a hit with the younger set, too, this Jesus of Nazareth. For teen-agers have always been excited by the unusual, and when they listened to Christ's words — well, they knew that in their midst was the King of the nonconformists! Why, you might just as well have tried to predict the direction of a football's bounce as what He might say next!

No alert teen living in Palestine could've failed to notice that after Jesus passed through a town, there were fewer people blind, deaf, crippled, and unhappy. His words were so mighty that those who listened and obeyed walked away with their lives changed.

In preparing this book, I asked many teens this question: "Do you think many young people were among those who were fascinated by Christ's parables. If so, why?"

Some outstanding answers were given me. One of the best was:

> One of the basic characteristics of youth is curiosity. Jesus had been talked about a great deal by the adults. He had healed many. . . . Conflicting stories were circulated as to who He really was. Some reported that He was the promised Messiah. Others said No. What could have been more exciting than to join the eager crowds that were always pressing Him? They would see for themselves. Surely the teen-agers were there. Nothing could have kept them away!

That student was right, wasn't she? Now here's the point: Are today's teens any different? In some ways. Your fashion styles, types of recreation, transportation, and system of education have changed. But basically, space-age youth share with all young people of history certain needs: love, security, acceptance, success, a proper relationship to their Creator, and knowledge of what comes after death.

And that is what the parables deal with. That is why they have never grown old. The parables are more up-to-date than tomorrow morning's newspaper, because they give workable and reliable solutions to the problems of every age. And no age has needed their help any more than the space age.

The Heavenly Father once said of Jesus, "This is my beloved son, in whom I am well pleased: hear ye him." If you do listen and become "a doer of the word and not a hearer only" then they'll count you among those of whom that student spoke, when she said, "Nothing could have kept them away!"

The King's Library

"And he spake many things unto them in parables. . . . Who hath ears to hear, let him hear."

— MATTHEW 13:3, 9

PART ONE

EXCITING EXAMINATIONS

I will hear what God the Lord will speak.
—Psalms 85:8

Is the Grass Greener? 1

LUKE 15:11-32 (Phillips), THE PRODIGAL SON

"Once there was a man who had two sons. The younger one said to his father, 'Father, give me my share of the property that will come to me.' So he divided up his property between the two of them. Before very long, the younger son collected all his belongings and went off to a foreign land, where he squandered his wealth in the wildest extravagance. And when he had run through all his money, a terrible famine arose in that country, and he began to feel the pinch. Then he went and hired himself out to one of the citizens of that country who sent him out into the fields to feed the pigs. He got to the point of longing to stuff himself with the food the pigs were eating, and not a soul gave him anything. Then he came to his senses and cried aloud, 'Why, dozens of my father's hired men have got more food than they can eat, and here am I dying of hunger! I will get up and go back to my father, and I will say to him: "Father, I have done wrong in the sight of Heaven and in your eyes. I don't deserve to be called your son any more. Please take me on as one of your hired men.'' So he got up and went to his father. But while he was still some distance off, his father saw him and his heart went out to him, and he ran and fell on his neck and kissed him. But his son said: 'Father, I have done wrong in the sight of Heaven and in your eyes. I don't deserve to be called your son any more. . . .' 'Hurry!' called out his father to the servants, 'fetch the best clothes and put them on him! Put a ring on his finger and shoes on his feet, and get that calf we've fattened and kill it, and we will have a feast and a celebration! For this is my son — I thought he was dead, and he's alive again. I thought I had lost him, and he's found!' And they began to get the festivities going."

"How old does a guy have to be before he can be his own boss?" asked a teen-age boy of his dad.

"I don't know, son," answered the father. "Nobody ever lived that long!"

You would have talked yourself hoarse trying to get that father's point across to the young man in this chapter's parable. He was "fed up to here" with rules. Tired of being told what to do, the boy wanted to do his own thing. He decided he would go away, where a guy could come and go as he pleased without having to watch the time or give explanations. The grass grows greener somewhere across those hills, imagined the boy. No "orders from headquarters" after a fellow changes his home address!

So begins the most famous story in all literature. You probably learned it years ago. It's called the parable of the prodigal son. Jesus Christ spoke it, and it contains some truths more exciting than the contents of diaries or opinion books!

Not the least of these attention getters is the father's attitude toward his son's wanting to leave. He didn't try to stop him. You don't have to be a member of the National Honor Society to know the boy's decision was the result of an ever-widening split in his relationship with his dad. Undoubtedly, the father had tried many times to explain the reason for rules and discipline, and that all he did where the boy was concerned was an expression of his love. But the explanations didn't sink in. After all, thought the prodigal, what could *he* know about this new generation? Times have changed; his old-fashioned ideas need walking canes and rocking chairs.

Why didn't the father *make* the boy stay home? Surely he knew the boy was headed for trouble. The boy's attitude earmarked him as "an accident looking for some place to happen." Was something wrong with the father, too? Did he really love the boy, if he *let* him leave home?

This is worth looking into. The father knew that the boy was headed for something far different from those exciting dreams of greener grass swirling in his youthful mind. He knew something else too — *love can't be forced.* If the boy had really loved him, he wouldn't have minded being an obedient son. Any youth who has ever been in love knows that pleasing the person he loves is not a duty; it's a delight. But the boy had lost his love for his dad. And more than anything else in the world, the father wanted his son's love.

After getting his share of the property, the son lost little time converting it into cash. A little later our young adventurer, his back pocket bulging and

21

suitcase in hand, walked away "foot loose and fancy free." Probably no thought of his broken-hearted father standing outside the old homestead watching him leave could push its way into his mind already filled with thoughts of "living it up." The prodigal never even looked back. The appeal of greener pastures can be terribly strong.

When he got to where he thought the grass grew greener (a foreign land), the prodigal lost no time in making friends — or should we say *buying* them? For as soon as his money ran out, his friends did, too. On top of that a famine engulfed the land and he "began to feel the pinch." Broke and hungry, the only job he could find was that of feeding pigs.

Feeding pigs! Greener grass? At first, on his own, things were "looking up." Now they were "breaking up." Little had he realized when he was foolishly "painting the town" that his actions were setting in motion bitter consequences which would catch up with him later on.

> He went out one full-mooned night,
> Thought he'd paint the town.
> He had no trouble living it up,
> But plenty living it down!

Fun or Folly?

In the midst of these miserable conditions, the youth was struck by a comparison and a realization. He compared what he had back home with what he had become stuck with. "Why, dozens of my father's hired men have more food than they can eat, and here I am dying of hunger!"

His realization? He had sought fun and freedom away from the father. What a joke! As he meditated, his life away from home marched before him in painful review: He was free to choose his friends, *until* they turned thumbs down on him as soon as he no longer served their purpose. He was free to do what he wanted, *until* his money (given him by the father) ran out. He was free to select his pleasures, *but* he could not select the consequences.

The freedom hunter learned the hard way that freedom to *do* never means freedom to *be*. Examples of this are many. You are *free* to take the easiest and shortest route to your diploma or degree, but you are *not free* to be as well prepared as you might have been. You are *free* to choose your friends, but *never free* to keep from becoming what they are. You are *free* to ignore your responsibilities to God, but *not free* to remain happy, guiltless, or safe as a result.

You can sooner find the last breath you breathed than freedom away from the Christ who speaks this parable to you. The prodigal became free from the father only to become a slave to himself, his passions, and selfish interests. It was a bitter pill to swallow, but he learned that "You belong to the power which you choose to obey, whether you choose sin, whose reward is death, or God, obedience to whom means the reward of righteousness."

The prodigal suddenly decided to quit yielding himself to the wrong master. His heart was aching for companionship with the father. A terrible loneliness and emptiness had gnawed all the "kicks" out of his life. (Parties, friends, projects, money, prestige — all lose their value quicker than an orchid corsage left too long in the sunshine, when sin has separated you from God.)

So he decided to go back. But not without admitting to himself that he'd "sinned against heaven and his father." This takes some doing. He didn't try to excuse himself because of his friends, his parents, the world's tension, modern teachings of off-color psychology. Not this boy! He had sinned! It pained him. He was ashamed, humiliated, and deeply sorry. You are probably acquainted with some whose attitude is quite different. They seem to think that they are doing the Lord of Heaven and earth a king-size favor by managing to be moral and mannerly when it's convenient. What works wonders with a loving God, however, is a bowed head, wet cheeks, and "be merciful to me a sinner."

Now get a load of the father's reaction when he sees the boy appear in the distance! Does he belly-laugh sarcastically and bellow, "Well, well, well! Don't tell me you couldn't succeed as a self-made man! Failed, didn't you? Well, it was exactly what you deserved!"

No, there's none of that. No "I told you so's." Instead the overjoyed father lovingly embraces his son, and throws a party!

Jesus spoke this parable to young people of that day and of every day to follow. No generation of teens was ever hungrier for its message of God's love than are teens of the space age. Jesus used this story to explain how much He loves *you.* Miracles take place when this is understood and believed. "The greatest happiness of our life," wrote Victor Hugo, "is the conviction that we are loved, loved not for ourselves, but rather loved in spite of ourselves." What did the prodigal do to deserve being forgiven? — and what can *we* do?

Knowledge of this parable will never again permit you to think that no one cares. Less than three years after He had given the world this story, Jesus was to *prove* how much he cared by dying on the cross — taking your place and mine, at Calvary. Although Christ had lived a perfect, sinless life, He made Himself the guiltiest man who ever lived by taking upon Himself your sins and mine. God showed that He approved that precious Sacrifice by raising His Son from the dead after three days. Every Easter is a reminder that you are loved by God so much that "He gave his only begotten Son that whosoever believeth on him should not perish, but have everlasting life."

Ought we not to get something more out of this than a puny "Somebody up there likes me"?

Greener grass? An exciting life? True freedom? These *are* possible if you do the right thing when you hear the Saviour saying, "I am the door: by me if any man [all teen-agers included!] enter in, he shall be saved, and shall go in and out and find pasture" (John 10:9). Any dedicated Christian teen can tell you that here are the greener pastures, the best times, the wide open spaces!

EXPRESS YOUR OPINION

1. Why did Jesus take an illustration of God's love for the lost from family life?

2. What does the foreign land represent?

3. What does *prodigal* mean?

4. Although prodigals can find Christ's love and forgiveness, what can be some of the possible effects of their influence on others while they are in the far country?

5. After the prodigal returned, do you think he ever had a desire to leave again? Why?

If You Want the Best 2

MATTHEW 13:44-46 (King James Version), THE
  HIDDEN TREASURE AND THE PEARL OF
  GREAT PRICE

"Again, the kingdom of heaven is like unto a
treasure hid in a field; the which when a man
hath found, he hideth, and for joy thereof goeth
and selleth all that he hath, and buyeth that field.

"Again, the kingdom of heaven is like unto a
merchant man, seeking goodly pearls: Who, when
he had found one pearl of great price, went and
sold all that he had, and bought it."

Being a Christian is like taking large doses of
castor oil — at least that's the impression some people seem to give. Those who mean better sometimes make young people think that Christians live
fun-starved "give up" experiences. They unwrap
their advice on how to live the thrilling Christian
life with comments such as, "you must give this
up," or "let that go."

Against that "quit," "don't," "stop" philosophy,
Jesus placed *His* idea of what it's really like to be-

come a privileged member of His Kingdom. "The Kingdom of heaven is like unto treasure hid . . . the which when a man hath found, he . . . *for joy thereof* goeth and selleth *all that he hath and buyeth. . . .*"

The Parable Preacher could have stopped there, but another parable containing something too good to keep quiet about, had to be told. "Again," continued Jesus, "the kingdom of heaven is like unto a merchant man, seeking goodly pearls: who, when he hath found one pearl of great price, went and *sold all that he had,* and bought it."

Couldn't they have been young men, these two that Jesus was talking about? After all, it's during youth that the spade is picked up and the great search for life's meaning begins. Many are digging and searching without having much success. If this continues too long, life can lose all its luster and appeal. A "what's the use" attitude may result.

When the spade does strike the secret, or the pearl is found, it is not what lots of teens expect it to be. To them, hitting life's jackpot means gaining scads of popularity, indulging in "whatever the gang decides," exercising power over others, or "getting what I want." But when these are tested for their staying power and ability to satisfy over an entire lifetime, their shallow sparkle fades quicker than cheap sportswear after the first washing.

These two men of whom Jesus spoke had three characteristics which set them apart from the crowd. They will set you apart, too, if you possess them.

1. They knew when they had made an important discovery. In his late teens a young man

named Galileo was sitting in a church in Pisa, Italy. A swinging oil lamp caught his eye. Others had seen it before. He had, too, but never like this! The discovery he made that day was to shatter two thousand years of tradition and help furnish the cornerstone of the modern science of dynamics, a branch of physics dealing with motion and force.

You are to be commended if nobody has succeeded in making you believe that the he-men pass up the pearl and the kids in the "top ten" sneer at the hidden treasure. Few mid-twentieth century teens openly oppose Jesus and His church, but how many do you know who get upset unless they are enjoying Christ's approval on their every decision and act?

The modern attitude toward the value of Christ comes nearer to being, "Oh, He was a good man; I'm sure He meant well," than "My eternal destiny depends upon the way I believe in Him." Don't be taken in by underhanded slander campaigns aimed at belittling the value of being a Christian. Some are not the least bit bashful in telling you, "Pansies and social cast-offs are the only ones who need to take Christianity seriously. Brains and beauties don't have to *resort* to religion."

If they only knew! Nothing else in life gives you as much reason for wanting to "kick up your heels" as knowing that your sins are forgiven and that you are loved and led daily by the Lord Jesus Christ. And every teen will be given a chance to discover Him. Your chance will come. Maybe it already has. Could it be facing you now?

2. These two men had another characteristic in common: They desired their discovery so greatly, that each man gladly sold all he had to purchase

it. There's not even a hint of hesitation or reluctance to get the "find" at any cost. They were too smart to want to keep the good when they could have the best!

"But surely we're not to get this 'worked-up' over Christianity," think the reserved (who are really the indifferent!). And you know that not many of your classmates are seen turning cartwheels over their faith. Many of them think that accepting Christ as Saviour and Lord would subtract everything enjoyable from their life. Their favorite term for those who do "sell all" is "fanatic." (A fanatic has been defined as someone who loves Jesus more than you do!)

It wasn't until a very attractive blonde joined Johnny's Sunday school class that he started exercising greater care with his dress. Dressing up suddenly became a pleasure!

Sandra never could get interested in math, until she discovered that money problems were a major cause of marital problems. Because she wanted to be the best wife possible some day in the future, Sandra began diligently to apply herself.

Imposition or Acquisition

Nobody feels "put out" at doing what is necessary to achieve a highly desirable goal. Being a Christian is not a matter of how much you have to give up, can't do, or where you can't go. The truth of the matter is this: You don't give up a thing when you decide to become a Christian. You *exchange* those things of inferior value for Jesus, the Hidden Treasure and Pearl of Great Price.

And what bargains! Your sin for His Salvation! Your time for His eternity! Your bitterness for His love! When you see Jesus — really see Him as loving you personally — you, like the two men in the parables, won't mind selling all, either! For with Him you have everything; without Him you have nothing, no matter what else you have.

Those who see only the can'ts and don'ts of Christianity reject it. "Imposition!" they protest. Others see the supreme value of the Christ. "Acquisition!" they exclaim . . . and willingly sell all they have — time, talents, energy, influence, and personal desires — to acquire it. And this is what it costs!

3. The last characteristic held in common by our two leading men was that each man followed through on his decision to make the purchase. It was a decision based on the value of the discovery and not their excited feelings. You don't come to know Christ because you get emotional. You get emotional (in your own way) *after* you have found Him, or *because* you have found Him! Emotion is never an introduction to Christ; it's a reaction to meeting Him.

Modern times claim Dr. Albert Schweitzer as one of its truly great men. As a brilliant youth, he earned the doctor's degree in philosophy, music, medicine and theology. When most young men are trying to decide what they want to do, Dr. Schweitzer was already the author of widely praised books in philosophy and theology. He had an incredibly promising future.

Then he met Christ! He saw that in Jesus his life could be changed and given purpose, which he hadn't had before. He decided to commit his life to his Lord. His decision carried him to Lambrene, in French Equatorial Africa, about fifty miles below the equator. After clearing the forests and erecting a makeshift hospital, Dr. Schweitzer began his medical missionary work among the natives. Now his work is known around the world, because he "sold all he had" and gladly gave his life for the glory of Jesus Christ.

A Swiss legend tells about a shepherd boy who discovered a rare flower one day while watching his sheep. Noticing the flower's radiant colors and the beauty of its design, he could not resist picking it up. As he did, he heard a noise, and looking around, saw the side of a nearby mountain roll back. Instantly, a dazzling reflection of the mountain's interior was exposed.

The boy rushed into the mountain and to his amazement saw what caused the reflection. The sun had fallen upon a great mass of precious jewels and stones! Laying aside the flower, the boy began filling his pockets with the largest and most precious of all the jewels. Then a voice startled him, saying, "Don't forget the best." The boy looked around but couldn't see anyone. So after picking up all he could carry, he walked outside, leaving the flower behind.

Suddenly, the side of the mountain rolled shut and to his dismay, the boy saw that all his jewels had turned to dust. Again, the voice spoke, "You forgot the best — the flower." Without the flower the treasure was lost.

The most wide-awake teens in this rapidly moving space age are those who "haven't forgotten the flower" — Jesus Christ. They have remembered to seek the Lord "in the days of their youth." Their decision keeps them from being tied to puny second bests. They understand, too, that deciding to "sell all" is tough when the value of salvation is seen through smut-covered glasses. It is, then, easier

32

to accept life's inferior side than to stay in bed late Saturday mornings.

You don't have to be honor roll material to know life offers you values "marked down." Girls who are "easy" do enjoy a certain kind of popularity. Grades can be raised by a certain kind of craftiness and straying eyes. And certain friendships can be maintained by turncoating on what Mom, Dad and your Sunday school teacher taught you.

There *are* certain kinds of values to be found in life's bargain basement. But are they bargains when you have to go *down* to get them . . . ? Isn't it time we realized that we're made with built-in space suits? We can stand a higher life! Jesus said, "Where your treasure is, there will your heart be also." No wonder so many teens have set their affections on things above!

EXPRESS YOUR OPINION

1. Which of the two parables in this chapter tells the story of most Christian youth you personally know?

2. How can you tell when a teen has really seen the value of accepting Christ?

3. Why don't more youth see the value of salvation?

4. Are there dangers in requiring those who want to accept Christ to begin immediately doing what your church traditions and customs demand?

Sooner Try Holding Back a Hurricane! 3

MARK 4:26-32 (The New English Bible), THE MUSTARD SEED AND THE YEAST

"He said, 'The kingdom of God is like this. A man scatters seeds on the land; he goes to bed at night and gets up in the morning, and the seed sprouts and grows — how, he does not know. The ground produces a crop by itself, first the blade, then the ear, then full-grown corn in the ear; but as soon as the crop is ripe, he plies the sickle, because harvesttime has come.'

"He said also, 'How shall we picture the kingdom of God, or by what parable shall we describe it? It is like the mustard-seed, which is smaller than any seed in the ground at its sowing. But once sown, it springs up and grows taller than any other plant, and forms branches so large that the birds can settle in its shade.'"

MATTHEW 13:33 (The New English Bible)

"He told them also this parable: 'The kingdom of Heaven is like yeast, which a woman took and mixed with half a hundredweight of flour till it was all leavened.'"

DID YOU EVER JOIN a club or organization of any kind only to see it fold up? Sort of makes you feel like a balloon after all the air has leaked out, doesn't it? The uhhh following the whoosh! — What a letdown!

You can well understand why the people who sat listening to this amazing man named Jesus were using caution. Although membership in Jesus' company looked very promising indeed, it was only natural to wonder about the wisdom of taking such a step. Being a charter member is an honor *if* the organization succeeds. Otherwise, a fellow may become the laughing stock of the neighborhood. And so Jesus proceeded to explain that the kingdom of God — what He was bringing into the world — was not a fly-by-night get-together.

Even the youth in the crowd understood what Jesus meant when He used the seed to illustrate His point. Once the seed is planted, cultivation may aid its development, but it sprouts and grows "[man] knows not how." Man has nothing to do with that process. And that is what the kingdom of God is like, Jesus taught. Man may plan, organize and promote, but God is the One who will make it grow and spread.

This ought to take the doubt out of every unbeliever and the whine from every discouraged Christian. No matter what the headlines scream, "He's got the whole world in His hands." Christianity will not succeed because of trial and error testings, or human cleverness. The Kingdom will take root and grow because the King has charge of it!

And don't underestimate His power to do the job. Space-age citizens need to realize that a strong voice from Scotland (James Stewart) spoke the truth when he said:

> Do let us be clear that what as Christians we celebrate is not a human genius who went about continually doing good, teaching wonderful lessons on the Fatherhood of God and the brotherhood of man, and holding views on ethics and international politics far in advance of His time. That would never have crashed into the throne of Caesar and routed the darkness of the world. That is a poor, insipid imitation of the dynamic and explosive thing the New Testament is talking about. What the New Testament bears witness to on every page, what carried the message like a prairie fire across the world, was no such dwarfed and timid version of the Gospel. It was the astounding fact that in Jesus of Nazareth the ultimate and eternal had struck down into history and broken through into the life of men.

The Outside and Inside of It

To illustrate how the Kingdom looks externally, the Master Teacher used the mustard seed. From extremely small seed, the mustard plant grows so large that birds can light on its branches. So will God's reign in human hearts grow from a small beginning to a world-wide order.

Christ's good news has caught fire in the hearts of people, young and old, wherever it has been taught. The result? Churches, hospitals, schools and institutions benefiting mankind are erected. All around us are the visible signs that "the Kingdom is like a mustard seed."

The internal growth of the Kingdom is compared to leaven, or yeast, as your home economics teacher would call it. Even when external proof of the growth of the Kingdom is hard to see, there is going on an internal work. Christ's Spirit is working in the hearts of teens today. School newspaper reporters and poll takers may not know it, but there are those teens who "have ears to hear."

Responsive ears hear and responsive hearts obey. There, in a small church, a teen-ager hears Christ's call. He remains faithful to his youth group. He may be the only boy who does, but he does. In another town a certain teen-age girl breaks off her dating relationship with a boy of questionable character. To continue going with him would mean to compromise a newly found concept of the human body as being the temple of the Holy Spirit, and therefore, to be kept pure. Somewhere else, the spirit of the Lord falls upon a youth group and makes incredibly real the person of Jesus in their midst. Immediately thereafter, Bible reading becomes preferred literature, prayer an elevating conversation with Christ, and witnessing a pleasure.

And so while you read this, His kingdom is growing. God hasn't shouted it from a P.A. system in space or declared it in blazing letters across the heavens. He has told us in simple stories that speak to and light up the heart.

Now . . . near you . . . across town . . . in another state . . . beyond the seas . . . the Holy Spirit is at work, powerfully, quietly, and continuously. Somewhere a teen hears a sermon or reads an explosive message from the Bible and falls in love with the crucified and resurrected Speaker of the parables. No bands play, no headlines carry the news, no motorcade takes him down main street (who needs this, when the angels in heaven have taken notice!). Despite the lack of earthly fanfare, the boy influences another teen to strike up a similar romance. And that teen wins another. And on it goes and grows.

Not so sensational? But, so sure! Not very dramatic, but very definite. Will it work? Some sophisticated youth unfamiliar with the Master's techniques have doubted it. Maybe it does lack the emotional impact of a pep rally and the "everybody's doing it slogan." However, just because its beginning showed no more promise than a mustard seed and its workings are as silent as yeast, don't sell God's kingdom short. God's cause in the world will go over — big! And He will see to it without having to turn up the volume.

Anyway, do things *have* to be noisy to be nice? What's quieter than light? But it works, doesn't it? Since when has the moon had to shout to quicken the hearts of lovers?

Yes, according to Jesus, the way the Christian army gets its recruits is unusual, but it will grow and triumph. Sooner try to pull a fistful of lightning from the sky, or hold back a hurricane with the palm of your hand than try to prevent the "spendid society" from showing forth the glory of God to the ends of the earth!

EXPRESS YOUR OPINION

1. Is there any difference between the kingdom of God and the kingdom of Heaven? Compare Matthew 19:23, Mark 10:23 and Luke 18:24.

2. Can you make up a modern illustration Jesus might give if He were to speak to your youth group on the growth of His kingdom? Give it a try and submit it to your class for discussion.

3. How important is it to youth to know that Christ's program will succeed?

4. How responsible should youth feel in building the kingdom of God?

5. How do chapters three and four compare with each other?

You've Got It! 4

MATTHEW 25:14-30 (King James Version), THE
TALENTS

"FOR THE KINGDOM OF HEAVEN is as a man traveling
into a far country, who called his own servants,
and delivered unto them his goods. And unto one
he gave five talents, to another two, and to another one; to every man according to his several
ability; and straightway took his journey. Then
he that had received the five talents went and
traded with the same, and made them other five
talents. And likewise he that had received two,
he also gained other two. But he that had received one went and digged in the earth, and hid
his lord's money.

"After a long time the lord of those servants cometh, and reckoneth with them. And so he that had
received five talents came and brought other five
talents, saying, Lord, thou deliveredst unto me
five talents: behold, I have gained beside them
five talents more. His lord said unto him, Well
done, thou good and faithful servant: thou hast
been faithful over a few things, I will make thee

41

ruler over many things: enter thou into the joy of thy lord.

"He also that had received two talents came and said, Lord, thou deliveredst unto me two talents: behold, I have gained two other talents beside them. His lord said unto him, Well done, good and faithful servant; thou hast been faithful over a few things, I will make thee ruler over many things: enter thou into the joy of thy lord.

"Then he which had received the one talent came and said, Lord, I knew thee that thou art an hard man, reaping where thou hast not sown, and gathering where thou hast not strawed: And I was afraid, and went and hid thy talent in the earth: lo, there thou hast that is thine. His lord answered and said unto him, Thou wicked and slothful servant, thou knewest that I reap where I sowed not, and gather where I have not strawed: Thou oughtest therefore to have put my money to the exchangers and then at my coming I should have received mine own with usury. Take therefore the talent from him, and give it unto him which hath ten talents. For unto every one that hath shall be given, and he shall have abundance: but from him that hath not shall be taken away even that which he hath. And cast ye the unprofitable servant into outer darkness: there shall be weeping and gnashing of teeth."

YES, YOU'VE GOT IT! . . . Talent, that is, and it's the stuff pros are made of, no less!

Whether you realize it or not, you have been cut from high quality cloth. No matter what your family's bank account or background amounts to, you came into this world with abilities built in.

There are no exceptions. *"Every man* hath his proper gift of God. . . ."* We are given a thought-provoking illustration of this in the parable of the talents. In this parable three men were given talents and instructed to use them. One of these three men represents *you*; the Master who gave them, Jesus Himself.

What is a talent? You won't find the following definition in your dictionary, but it is Biblically based and has the Christian perspective in it. A talent may be thought of as the ability which, when used in Jesus' name, enables you to be of service to others to the glory of God.

And mark the day when an awareness of your talents leaps into your conscious mind! It is no small thrill to discover that you can write persuasive paragraphs, play a musical instrument or hit a baseball 350 feet!

Unless a sharp eye is used, danger can creep in with the awakening of slumbering talents. Making comparisons is one form this danger takes. Because we sometimes classify the value of talents according to the number of people who see them in operation, we can develop what the freshman psychology text calls "complexes." For example, if your talents fail to measure up to those of some teen who can wow them either from behind the speaker's stand or on the athletic field, you can get an inferiority complex. True, no one should think higher of himself than he ought. But if your feelings of inadequacy are so strong that you are robbed of your desire to achieve, you will be a benchwarmer in life's game forever. This saddens the very heart of God, for as Dr. Charles L. Allen has said, "God looks at every man with two eyes, the eye of forgiveness and the eye of expectation."

43

On the other hand, comparing your talents with those of another whose talents are exercised behind the scenes can give you a superiority complex. And "stuck up" people are less popular than a fresh crop of pimples!

The safe course to steer is this: compare your efforts to achieve today with yesterday's best. You might define progress as competing today with your best yesterday and coming out on top.

Realize, too, that all talents are not to be thought of as intellectual, athletic, musical, artistic, etc. These *publicly* exercised talents draw the applause of society and get front page coverage in newspapers. But don't get the idea you are not talented because you've never made the honor roll, scored a touchdown, played in a school band or created beautiful landscapes. Jesus makes this very clear. *Everybody* has his own unique strength, gifts and advantages. You have been created as uniquely as a fingerprint. God wants to use your uniqueness for His glory!

Inspiration or Perspiration

Another danger which talented teens must be on the lookout for is that of misunderstanding the nature of talents. They never spring out fully developed at some magical moment. Although given you by your Creator, your talents have to be developed by *you* — even *after* conversion! This takes time, planning, patient effort, and overcoming failure. A famous writer once said, "When I was a young man, I observed that nine out of ten things I did were failures. I didn't want to be a failure, so I did ten times more work." Talent alone will get you nowhere; the developing and exercising of it as unto God is what makes the difference. Inspiration without perspiration is of little value. "A diamond," someone has noted, "is a piece of coal that stuck with it."

When the talent giver in our story returned, he wanted to know what had been going on during his absence. The two men who received five and two talents respectively had doubled what had been given them. We who have fewer talents than others ought to get a tremendous charge out of reading that both men got the *same* reward!

> *His Lord said unto him, well done thou good and faithful servant: Thou hast been faithful over a few things, I will make thee ruler over many things: enter thou into the joy of thy Lord.*

Did our eyes deceive us? Did we really read where the number of talents made no difference to the Lord? They were called "good" and "faithful." It was not what the men had, but what they *were* that caused the needle to swing on God's applause meter! This goes across the grain of the philosophy of most of the people we know who are trying desperately "to get ahead." To them goodness and faithfulness to God are all right — so long as it puts them before the right people and doesn't cramp their style. Rather than being good and faithful, they prefer to be popular and clever.

Use Them or Lose Them

What about the man who received one talent? He had tried to do nothing with his talent and had succeeded admirably! He simply buried his talent. He could have thrown up any number of reasons for his actions (or the lack of them). "If I can't have as much talent as _____, I'll just do nothing!" "Nobody bragged on me, when I tried, so that's that!" "Oh, well, what I can do is so unimportant, nobody will notice if I drop out." Whatever his excuses were, the master would have none of them. "Take therefore the talent from him. . . ."

No place here for a "ho hum" attitude toward the development of our abilities! Ask any bodybuilder what happens if he takes too long a layoff. The message is clear, regarding our talents: We use them or lose them. Their number and kind matter little — to God. He wants our love and faithfulness before our talents, personality, and service, anyway. The "apple of our Lord's eye" is *first* good and faithful. *Then* he's concerned about his gifts.

Christian youth, glowing with desire to please their Lord, will consecrate themselves to the task (don't expect it to be easy!) of making the most out of what they have been given. They realize the poet was right when he said:

> It isn't by size that you win or you fail —
> Be the best of whatever you are!

And so this you must know: God has created you for a purpose. So that you can accomplish this purpose, He had given you special abilities. Or should we say "given"? Would it be closer to the truth to say He *lends* us our gifts for a lifetime. . . ?

A day is coming when He will want to know what you did with what He has given you. The late Fritz Kreisler, one of the world's great violinists, once said, "I have never opened my violin case, I have never touched a bow in my life without offering them as a gift back to God." This

46

wonderful concept was perfectly caught by a senior class that chose for its motto:

> What you are is God's gift to you,
> What you become is your gift to God.

When Christ-centered love and developed skill get together in your life, a masterpiece will result! And you might be surprised to know what you can do, believing as Paul, who said, "I can do all things through Christ which strengtheneth me" (Phil. 4:13).

EXPRESS YOUR OPINION

1. Does this parable teach that everybody is *not* created equal?

2. Does this parable have something to say to those who claim "I don't have time to read, practice," etc.?

3. What effect on your talents do your family life, church, school and social life have?

4. Are your talents and interests and God's will for your life related to each other? How? Why?

5. Discuss how the parable of the talents relates to the parable of the prodigal son.

PART TWO

REMARKABLE QUALIFICATIONS

Every good gift and every perfect gift is from above, and cometh down from the Father. . . .

—James 1:17

Not Everything's Coming Up Roses, But ... 5

MATTHEW 13:24-30 (King James Version), THE TARES

"ANOTHER PARABLE PUT HE FORTH unto them, saying, The kingdom of heaven is likened unto a man which sowed good seed in his field: But while men slept, his enemy came and sowed tares among the wheat, and went his way. But when the blade was sprung up, and brought forth fruit, then appeared the tares also. So the servants of the householder came and said unto him, Sir, didst not thou sow good seed in thy field? from whence then hath it tares? He said unto them, An enemy hath done this. The servants said unto him, Wilt thou then that we go and gather them up? But he said, Nay; lest while ye gather up the tares, ye root up also the wheat with them. Let both grow together until the harvest: and in the time of harvest I will say to the reapers, Gather ye together first the tares, and bind them in bundles to burn them: but gather the wheat into my barn."

HER ARM WAS BLACK AND BLUE and quite swollen.

As she talked, the unpleasant picture of this teen-ager's family life came more clearly into focus. First, there was the divorce of her parents. Then the remarriage of her mother, with whom she lived. To top it all, the stepfather had a fierce temper, of which he often lost control, and of which his step-children were the unfortunate victims. All this was confirmed by an adult who was well acquainted with the family.

Other teens with problems equally as distressing have talked with me during my years of teaching in the Houston, Texas, public schools and in youth camps across the nation.

Reasoning and Wrestling

At about fifteen years of age your ability to reason matures. Of course, your *judgment* hasn't matured, but it will as your experience and training continue. Nevertheless, you are beginning to see life and its complications as never before. For life, you are discovering, doesn't always pat you; it can punch you, too — hard!

The maturing teen is no longer taken in by life, masquerading in bright colors and false faces. Let a death take place in the family — or a sickness linger on and on — or a greatly desired scholarship be denied — or a trusted friend betray your confidence, and Job's complaint makes sense: "Man born of woman is of few days and full of trouble."

Why all the trouble in life? Who's responsible for it? What can you do about it? Weighty questions, these! And they are dealt with in the parable of the tares.

Treating Not Retreating

"Let's not talk about it and maybe it'll go away"

was never Jesus' way of handling troublesome topics. Those who know Him have learned that Jesus never dodges the issue. This parable proves that Christ always treated life as it was and is. No little comfort is gotten from knowing that Christ can be trusted to be realistic.

In this parable Jesus teaches us that "not everything's coming up roses." The enemy has brought evil (the tares) into the world. Who is this enemy? Don't look for the answer in the top ten best sellers or any of your science textbooks. So-called intellectuals might grin at the idea, but Jesus unhesitatingly tells us it's the devil. And today's teens could do worse than to give some thought to Christ's warning to Peter, concerning the devil's reality and intentions: "Oh, Simon, Simon, behold, Satan hath desired to have you, that he might sift you as wheat. But I have prayed for thee, that thy faith fail not" (Luke 22:31, 32). Another sobering verse, I Peter 5:8, says: "Be self-controlled and vigilant always, for your enemy the devil is always about, prowling like a lion roaring for its prey."

"Man's inhumanity to man" has not stopped. The devil hasn't let the new frontier scare him away. We who are blessed beyond measure to live in "the land of the free and the home of the brave" still must be aware of prejudices, ignorance, crime, and sin of all types. If you think about the evils *too* much, however, and forget your blessings, you might share the following opinion:

> God's plan made a hopeful beginning;
> But man spoiled his chances by sinning
>   We trust that the story
>   Will end in God's glory,
> But at present, the other side's winning.

But is it? Recall the power discussed in chapter 3? God hasn't thrown in the towel yet! Neither has He wandered off looking for new worlds to create while earth's people prepare to be swallowed up eventually by all the evil that's around us. One of Russia's astronauts declared he looked for God during his orbital flight, but didn't see Him. That's puny proof of atheistic arguments! There are still plenty of I. ....evers around who realize the world is God's classroom. He's never missed a day and is always there on time. Christian teens get peace of mind when they find out that concerning His presence with us, the Lord has a perfect attendance record! "I will never leave thee, nor forsake thee" (Heb. 13:5).

Our next question goes something like this: What are we to do about the evil in the world? Is it our responsibility to destroy it? That's what the servants in the parable thought. "Then would you have us go gather them?"

Surprisingly enough, the answer was, "No." Why? "For you might root up the wheat when you were gathering up the weeds." Again the tender side of our Lord is exposed. To spare one broken heart, to avoid one tragic case of mistaken identity, Jesus cautions us against unwisely leveling judgment at others. Evil and good can look alike and can be found together.

You don't have to look far to find this mixture of good and evil. Christian youth don't have to have twenty-one candles on their birthday cake to experience an inward tug-of-war between their sinful and spiritual natures.

> Within my earthly temple there's a crowd;
> There's one of us that's humble, one that's
>   proud;

There's one who's broken-hearted for sins;
There's one who unrepentant sits and
   grins;
There's one who loves his neighbor as him-
   self;
There's one who cares for naught but fame
   and pelf.
From such perplexities I would be free,
If I could once determine which is me!

After being asked to tell who the most outstanding figure in history was, one of my former students replied, "Everytime I think of a good man,
I think of something bad he's done." And this is
the sad but true commentary on mankind. Even
in church you will discover those who are less than
perfect after all. Even Christians can do wrong.
But they don't enjoy it! And that's one of the pri-
mary differences between the unbeliever and the
saint.

Some youth are discouraged by hypocrites in the
church. (If you need an excuse for not becoming
a Christian, this one is always handy!) One fellow
was complaining about this problem when he was
advised by a quick-minded friend: "If you ever
find a perfect church, don't *you* go in!"

"Why?"

"It will cease to be perfect when *you* enter!"

A London church found it necessary to post this
notice: "Not everyone who goes to this church is
converted. Watch your hat and coat!"

Evil is not only in ourselves and in the church;
it is obviously all around us. Crime has increased
to the extent that on the present basis, the average
American who lives to the age of seventy will be
the victim of at least one serious crime.

Are we to do *nothing* about this? Is this parable

55

trying to tell us that we are to be throw-rugs for evil to wipe its feet on? The answer is suggested in the famous serenity prayer:

> God grant me
> the serenity to accept the things I cannot change
> the courage to change the things I can
> and the wisdom to know the difference.

The parable of the tares assures us that Christ Himself will assume full and final responsibility for destroying the works of the devil. "The son of man shall send forth his angels, and they shall gather out of his kingdom all things that offend, and them which do offend, and them which do iniquity; and shall cast them into a furnace of fire: there shall be weeping and wailing and gnashing of teeth."

Jesus doesn't let the parable end on a sour note, however. In concludes with a glimpse of those who overcame the evil in the world by the power of Christ. "Then shall the righteous shine forth as the sun in the kingdom of their Father."

Remember when the going gets tough that Christ has promised not to let anything happen to you that you cannot take. Defeat, handicaps, sorrows cannot get you down unless you surrender to them. Trust in Christ to take care of those things in your life which might cause you to become discouraged and lose heart. Something usually turns up for the person who keeps on digging.

The sixteenth chapter of John is made to order for teens when trouble comes. It ends with Christ saying, "These things have I spoken unto you, that in me you might have peace. In the world you shall have tribulation; but be of good cheer;

I have overcome the world." Another verse which gives encouragement is I John 5:4: "For whatsoever is born of God overcometh the world: and this is the victory that overcometh the world, even our faith."

Sometimes life can seem harsh. Things happen and you wonder why. But Christ has already overcome *all* of life's hard knocks and He will give you the power to be a champion, too. Believe Him. Trust Him. Do what you think He'd have you do, no matter how you feel. He will work things out. He always has; He always will. You'll see. Meanwhile, keep this verse in mind: "To him that overcometh will I grant to sit with me in my throne, even as I also overcame, and am set down with my father in his throne" (Rev. 3:21).

Victorious Christian living is not only possible, it is *profitable*. As the songwriter put it, "Just one glimpse of Him in glory will the toils of life repay."

EXPRESS YOUR OPINION

1. Recent youth surveys point out a dangerous "give-up" attitude held by many young people. Does this parable have an answer?

2. What can teen-agers do to overcome the evil in their high schools? Read I John 4:1-4; 5:5.

3. What kind of difficulty seems to give Christian youth whom you know the most trouble?

4. Does this parable give Christians a good reason for being optimistic? Discuss.

5. Discuss how Acts 1:8 applies to this chapter.

Change Your Mirrors to Windows **6**

LUKE 10:25-37 (The New English Bible), THE GOOD SAMARITAN

"ON ONE OCCASION A LAWYER came forward to put this test question to him: 'Master, what must I do to inherit eternal life?' Jesus said, 'What is written in the Law? What is your reading of it?' He replied, 'Love the Lord your God with all your heart, with all your soul, with all your strength, and with all your mind; and your neighbour as yourself.' 'That is the right answer,' said Jesus; 'do that and you will live.'

"But he wanted to vindicate himself, so he said to Jesus, 'And who is my neighbour?' Jesus replied, 'A man was on his way from Jerusalem down to Jericho when he fell in with robbers, who stripped him, beat him, and went off leaving him half dead. It so happened that a priest was going down by the same road; but when he saw him, he went past on the other side. So too a Levite came to the place, and when he saw him went past on the other side. But a Samaritan who was making the journey came upon him and when he saw him was moved to pity. He went up and bandaged his wounds, bathing them with oil and wine. Then he lifted him on to his own beast, brought him to an inn, and looked after him there. Next day he produced two silver pieces and gave them to the inn-keeper, and said, "Look after him; and if you spend any more, I will repay you on the way back." Which of these three do you think was neighbour to the man who fell into the hands of the robbers?' He answered, 'The one who showed him kindness.' Jesus said, 'Go and do as he did.' "

HAVE YOU EVER SAT IN CLASS wanting to ask a question, but didn't? If you had only realized that teachers like inquisitive students, you would have been much more courageous. Teachers know that inquiring minds are filled with question marks. It's a mistake to think that you only expose your ignorance when you ask a question. For questions indicate mental effort, concentration, and individual pursuit of the truth.

Civilization has been shaken by great questions that spurred the curious to find the answers. Think of some of the great questions of history:

> "How can I live so as to please God?" asked Martin Luther, who led the world out of the dark ages of superstition and spiritual blindness to the knowledge that salvation is by faith alone.

> "Why do some people resemble their father, and other people their mother?" wondered Gregor Mendell, who discovered the Mendelian law for dominant and recessive traits.

> "Can sound travel over wire?" asked Alexander Graham Bell, who invented the telephone. The

parents of any teen very well knows, especially when they're expecting an important call.

We owe our present parable to a devilishly curious lawyer who asked the Lord the greatest question of life: "Master, what should I do to be sure of eternal life?" But the question was "loaded." The lawyer wasn't trusting, he was testing. Jesus' answer sent him in desperate search of a way to get off the hook. He snatched the word *neighbor* out of Christ's reply and put it at the end of an interrogative sentence: "And who is my neighbour?"

Before the smirk could form on his face, the lawyer suddenly found himself playing defense. For Jesus answered his question with a rather shocking story. It's called the parable of the good Samaritan, and is second in popularity only to the parable of the prodigal son.

"A certain man was going from Jerusalem to Jericho." Every thief in the area knew this twenty-mile stretch of rocky, mountainous road. Called the "bloody pass," the route was a "haven for hoodlums." And sure enough, the poor man was ambushed, robbed, and beaten in true gangland style and left bleeding by the side of the road.

But he was in luck — or so you would think. For a priest came walking by, but he "passed by on the other side." Before our open-mouthed surprise can change, a Levite, whose life was the church, appears. But seeing the dying man, he too "passed by on the other side."

Well! The poor guy's had it, if even the men of the church don't want to get involved.

But here comes a Samaritan.

A Samaritan! Quick glances were exchanged as

that word pricked the ears of those listening to Jesus. Samaritan! Why, this was the word the Jews reserved for their bitterest enemies. Samaritan! The Jews had a saying: "The only good Samaritan is a dead one."

The Samaritan sees the pitiful sight and is "moved with compassion." A sharp eye and soft heart — was Jesus trying to "get through" to me and you with prerequisites for being a good neighbor? He was showing us the secret of winning friends . . . , and winning over enemies, too! Be concerned about others! Self-centeredness reveals immaturity and produces selfish citizens. Others-centeredness reveals maturity and produces nice neighbors.

The razor-sharp edge of what He's getting at probes our prejudices. "Who is my neighbour" is a dead giveaway in the first place. Any youth who asks that is saying something like this: "Now Jesus, an up-and-coming teen has to be very careful in his choice of friends. After all, birds of a feather. . . . And something else, Lord, a youth with ambition and pride has to leave his inferiors to those on their own level. You know, for one's reputation's sake."

Facts and Fences

The wounded man, was he a certain color? From the right side of the tracks? A degree-holder? The good Samaritan realized what so many of us don't. Our neighbor is not fenced in — or fenced out — by racial, geographical, academic, denominational, social barriers. Our neighbor is that one who needs help.

Sounds easy, doesn't it? Just the kind of answer you would like to give for bonus questions on tough tests. "Duck soup" for Sunday school quizzes too! But stop a second before you chalk up a perfect score on this one, and take another look at "our neighbor is the one who needs help."

This is the song Solomon sings in another verse: "Withhold not good from them to whom it is due when it is in the power of thine hand to do it" (Prov. 3:27).

To whom *is* good due? Surely not to that catty blonde who sits next to you in history class? All that eye makeup! And that mod outfit, could it possibly hide a broken heart? And besides, her reputation! Just think what your friends might think if you were seen in *her* company!

And what about that guy in your classes who is visited more frequently by the truant officer than his Sunday school teacher? Can *that* kind of guy need your help? Can a life like that be worthwhile to Jesus even if it does have the smell of tobacco on its clothes? It might be very interesting to get God's opinion on which is worse: far-out fashions and tobacco, or a "holier than thou" attitude.

The Samaritan administered first aid and then provided for the victim's room and board while he recuperated. This is Christianity going all the way. Help that is genuinely Christian walks the "second mile." Notice, too, that the Samaritan didn't take the man home with him. God doesn't expect us to shoulder the responsibility of taking every needy person into our home, or giving him all our money and all our time. You're not playing the role properly if you do someone's homework for him. Slipping the answers to the test to a "needy" student is not the idea. Helping others doesn't mean "stand back, let me do it for you." Rather it means, "move over and I'll give you a hand." The best kind of help is that which enables the victim to learn to help himself. This is possible if we can guide him to Christ who will start with him as he is, and then help him to complete recovery.

A legend tells of a man caught in quicksand. Confucious saw him and remarked, "There is evidence men should stay out of such places." Buddha came by and said, "Let that life be a lesson to the rest of the world." Mohammed observed him and said, "Alas, it is the will of Allah." A Hindu said, "Cheer up, friend, you will return to earth in another form." But when Jesus saw him He said, "Give me your hand, brother, and I will pull you out."

So the good Samaritan can represent Christ, too!

This parable covers a lot more ground than appears at first glance. With this simple story, Jesus explains the true reason for and the work of doctors, nurses, teachers, psychiatrists, social workers — all ministers to human needs. The good Samaritan lives today in every kind act, every encouraging word and every attempt at peacemaking.

But just a second. Before we go overboard applauding the parable's hero and back-slapping him to the tune of "for he's a jolly good fellow" let's hear the parable's punch line: "You go and do the same."

This is asking too much of those whose tiny world is lined with mirrors. Their only thoughts are of "me, myself and I." The population of their world is one — and they're it! But they miss out on knowing the incomparable joy of changing mirrors to windows, looking away from themselves to others and being of service to those whom they can help for the only acceptable reason — you love Christ and therefore love His creation.

Love makes possible great discoveries. A young man in love gets credit for having part in one of the greatest inventions in the history of mankind. This very book you hold in your hands owes Laurence Janzoon's romance a great debt. For while he daydreamed in Germany, during the 1420's — but let's let him tell it as he told it to a young man named Johannes Gutenburg:

> . . . I sometimes daydream under the willows by the canal. There I carve out the initials of my bride with my knife. Not on the bark of the trees, because I do not want anyone to see, but on blocks which I cut from the trunks of the willows.
>
> One day, when I had thus carved her initials on the green wood, they seemed better made than usual. I thought how pleased she would be if she saw them. So I wrapped the block in a piece of parchment and took it home. On opening the package the next day, I was astonished to see the initials imprinted on the brown parchment. The sap had oozed out and made the image!

And Gutenburg's idea for the printing press was born! For him the wounded man in the parable could have represented the ignorant and idea-starved people in the world.

The Jericho road stretches round the world. Everyone is walking it. How well you walk depends upon how you react to His instruction: "You go and do as he did."

EXPRESS YOUR OPINION

1. If Christ were talking to your youth group,

what race might the good Samaritan represent? Why do you think Jesus made villains out of the heroes (the priest and Levite) and a hero out of the villain (the Samaritan)?

2. Is it possible to be so "heavenly minded that you're no earthly good"? Explain.

3. Discuss Acts 8:26-59 in connection with this parable.

4. Many are faultfinders; a few are good Samaritans in that they notice the good qualities of others. What makes the difference?

5. Can an unbeliever be the kind of good Samaritan the Lord is talking about? Discuss.

You Won't Study This in Economics Class **7**

MATTHEW 20:1-16 (King James Version), THE LABORERS

"FOR THE KINGDOM OF HEAVEN is like unto a man that is an householder, which went out early in the morning to hire laborers into his vineyard. And when he had agreed with the laborers for a penny a day, he sent them into his vineyard. And he went out about the third hour, and saw others standing idle in the marketplace, And said unto them; Go ye also into the vineyard, and whatsoever is right I will give you. And they went their way. Again he went out about the sixth and ninth hour, and did likewise. And about the eleventh hour he went out, and found others standing idle, and saith unto them, Why stand ye here all the day idle? They said unto him, Because no man hath hired us. He saith unto them, Go ye also into the vineyard; and whatsoever is right, that shall ye receive.

"So when even was come, the lord of the vineyard saith unto his steward, Call the laborers, and give them their hire, beginning from the last unto the first. And when they came that were hired about the eleventh hour, they received every man a penny. But when the first came, they supposed that they should have received more; and they likewise received every man a penny. And when they had received it, they murmured against the good man of the house, Saying, These last have wrought but one hour, and thou hast made them equal unto us, which have borne the burden and heat of the day. But he answered one of them, and said, Friend, I do thee no wrong: didst not thou agree with me for a penny? Take that thine is, and go thy way: I will give unto this last, even as unto thee. Is it not lawful for me to do what I will with mine own? Is thine eye evil, because I am good? So the last shall be first, and the first last: for many be called, but few chosen."

HIGH SCHOOL STUDENTS in Charlotte, North Carolina, were polled on the question, Do you agree that the fairest economic system takes from each according to his ability, and gives to each according to his need? Thirty-seven percent of the students voted Yes.

Those who voted, No, were sharp enough to consider such questions as, How will the economic system determine the needs of each of its citizens? Who will decide what the abilities of each are? If you can't produce, what then? Will you be worthless to the system? Won't those who are capable of high productivity lose their desire to create, plan and work if much of what they earn is taken away and given to others who may be "gold-bricking"? Will the ambitious lose their ambition? Will the ne'er-do-wells ride the gravy train?

A "what's in it for me" attitude may be helpful in exposing communism's economic system as phony, but when Peter expressed it to Jesus, his ear must have burned when the answer was given.

"Lo, we have left everything and followed you," Peter said to Jesus one day. "What shall we have?" To answer Peter, Jesus compares Himself to an employer who gets up early one morning to hire workers to work in his vineyard. At nine o'clock in the morning he hires some more. This happens at noon, three o'clock and again at five o'clock. All the workers agreed to work for the same wage, a penny a day. Nobody grumbled, nobody complained.

At six o'clock the workers lined up for their pay checks. The men who had been working all day watched as those who had worked only one hour *got the same wage as they were to get!* Complaints to the boss were sudden and bitter. "These last have worked but one hour, and you have made them equal to us, who have borne the burden and the heat of the day."

The master reminded them of their original deal. "Friend, I do thee no wrong: didst thou not agree with me for a penny? . . . Is it not lawful for me to do what I will with mine own? Is thine eye evil because I am good?"

Keep in mind Peter's original question; otherwise this parable shrivels to nonsense. Peter wanted to know what the rewards are for living Jesus' brand of life. Jesus' answer is ridiculous if we let the *amount of wages* sidetrack us. You can sleep through most of your economics class and still know that if two people are doing the same work, one should get more pay if he works longer hours.

Since that is not true in this story, Jesus must have *deliberately* planned it that way to call our attention to something else. What could it be?

Perhaps this. Producing tally sheets, strenuous schedules (even church work schedules) or straight "A" report cards doesn't impress or obligate God. He is so big He doesn't have to make deals. Heaven will be cheap at any price. Knowing this, we are not to concern ourselves with how much we do, or the amount of our paycheck here on earth. We are to be so overjoyed at getting an opportunity to work for the Lord that our enthusiasm bubbles over, drowning all thoughts of "now what will I get for this?"

That is what Jesus is saying to us. The teen-age Christian, loving his Lord, realizes that working for God is not a bore, but a bargain; not a pain, but a pleasure! In fact it's the only work in the world worth getting this excited about.

O.K., O.K., so you *do* know lots of supposedly Christian young people who gripe because they *have* to go to church, who complain when they're asked to participate in the church program, who are reluctant to give their 10 percent, etc. Yes, there is quite a group like this. (Are you and am I always eager to do what we're asked to do for Christ?)

A Foreigner in the Family

If we dare, we can see ourselves (unhappy sight it is, too) in the parable of the elder brother. This one is normally used with the parable of the prodigal son. Tacked on here, its meaning is brought in sharp focus.

Remember the final scene in the parable of the

prodigal? His homecoming erupted in a celebration. We left them "having a ball."

Then big brother appears, grimy with sweat and dirt. He had been working all day in the field. Jerking his thumb in the direction of the house, he wants to know, "What's *that* all about?" When he's told of his little brother's return, does he hip-hip-hooray? No. All he can think of is the fact that he's never left home and "nobody ever gave me a party." His real purpose for staying home "like a good boy" is revealed. Sure, *he* stayed at home, but why? For what he could get out of it. He had been unable to learn that working for the Father is so noble a task, so great a privilege that you become unaware of whether your work is drawing raves from the pastor and press notices in the church bulletin.

The story doesn't end with everybody living happily ever after. The big brother's heart is hard. He has been exposed for what he really is — and is not. This parable with a sad ending is packed with meaning for modern teens, especially those who are called Christian. Jesus has given a brilliant illustration to show how it is possible to drop coins in the collection plate every Sunday of the year, go through all the motions of serving Christ and still be out of fellowship with the heavenly Father.

Now every teen knows something of how this works in different areas of life. Many have experienced it at home. A quarrel, jealousy, or fear can rob a family of a feeling of togetherness. Each member may go right on with the business at hand, but everyone knows "there's something rotten in Denmark." Dating teens know that feeling when the romance cools. You can be together, but some-

71

thing is missing. Then too, regarding your relationship to God, you can be a runaway at heart even though you never leave home.

And so the tragedy of going from riches to rags is seen in the elder brother's loss of fellowship with his dad. Sure, he still had the family name, ate, slept and worked at home. But the proper relationship between father and son was gone.

This is true of every teen who serves in the program of the church for the purpose (hidden to others) of getting something — praise, friends, prestige — any kind of reward from men, instead of giving all he's got to the Master's service because he loves the Master!

In this star-studded society of Christians, not everyone is a member who looks and acts like one. "Not everyone that saith Lord, Lord, shall enter into the kingdom of heaven."

Those who get Christ's approval and fellowship understand this! More important than what you do is your reason for doing it! It's not your actions but your attitude; not your service, but the spirit in which the service is performed, that classifies you in God's grade book.

David Livingston said, "People talk of the sacrifice I have made in spending much of my life in Africa. Can that be called a sacrifice which is simply paid back as a small part of a great debt owing to our God, which we can never repay? Is that a sacrifice which brings its own best reward in healthful activity, the consciousness of doing good, peace of mind, and a bright hope of a glorious destiny hereafter? Say rather, a privilege!"

EXPRESS YOUR OPINION

1. How important is enthusiasm in sports,

72

schoolwork, and on the job?

2. Should Christian service be done with as much enthusiasm as the activities listed in question 1?

3. Why do you think some Christian teens lack enthusiasm?

4. Are the parables of the buried treasure and pearl of great price related to the parable of the laborers? Explain.

5. Read Acts 16:23-25. Is it possible to match that kind of enthusiasm today? Can you?

How to Turn Over a New Leaf 8

MATTHEW 21:28-31 (Phillips), THE DECEITFUL SONS

"'BUT WHAT IS YOUR OPINION about this? There was a man with two sons. He went to the first and said, "Go and work in my vineyard today, my son." He said, "All right, sir" — but he never went near it. Then the father approached the second son with the same request. He said, "I won't." But afterward he changed his mind and went. Which of these two sons did what their father wanted?'"

"'The second one,'" they replied."

A NEW SEMESTER WAS beginning at Vicksboro High as Rex and his buddy, Hal, entered the crowded halls.

"Ole buddy, this semester you're gonna see some changes in yours truly," said Rex.

"Hear ye! Hear ye!" laughed Hal, shaking his head.

This was what Rex had expected. "Sounds like a familiar verse to a very old song, doesn't it?" he said. "But just stick around and watch my smoke."

"Got a magnifying glass?" kidded Hal.

Before Rex could answer, the bell summoned each boy to class. The frown that slowly replaced his smile indicated that Rex's mind was entertaining some troublesome thoughts. He was wondering if he really *could* turn over a new leaf. He'd tried before, but hadn't been able to keep it up for more than a week or two.

You and I know what Rex was facing, don't we? This problem of needing to change, of making a new start, is not limited to scholastic progress, either. It puts its long arms around the Christian's development, too.

Intentions and Decisions

Let's face it. No matter how good we are, we're still not good enough. It's hard to forget that we are classified with those of whom Paul spoke: "All have sinned and come short of the glory of God." This bothers every Christian teen, because it suggests a contradiction that seems impossible to explain. "How can I come short of the glory of God and still do the will of God? Is it possible to please God and still be less than perfect?"

Christ answers this question in a brief story called the parable of the deceitful sons. The parable tells of two boys who were asked by their father to spend the day working at home. One quickly snapped an obedient, Yes, sir! But he never went. The other son flatly refused with a stout, No. But afterwards he changed his mind and obeyed.

The first son made a great first impression, didn't he? He quickly put his best foot forward. For him this was good enough; actually, it should have been action in the planning stage. A fast, nice-sounding answer gave his conscience "instant relief." Chances are he was probably not a rebellious boy. He doesn't give us the idea that he's headed for juvenile court. Something more important came up and the father's instructions were merely forgotten. He intended to carry out his father's will, but was sidetracked before his breakfast had been digested.

Anybody can intend to turn over a new leaf, but how many can follow through? What you would *like* to do and what you *labor* to do may be farther apart than most of last year's "steadies." Over and over the Bible warns that it's not the one who starts out "but he that endureth to the end shall be saved" (Matt. 10:22). Other verses deserving close attention are: "If you are faithful to what I have said, you are truly my disciples" (John 8:31, Phillips) and "You must go on growing in me and I will grow in you" (John 15:4, Phillips).

We get the picture, don't we? A good beginning for Christ must outlast the weekend after the youth crusade or the summer youth camp. But what does this require? A perfect life from the time you first accept Jesus Christ as Saviour, until body and soul part? If so, we're all in hot water. Remember? "*All* have sinned and come short. . . ."

Our Life and His Love

In counseling teens in youth camps, this problem rises head and shoulders above most of the others. "It's no use," they say. "I tried to live the Christian life, but I failed. I just couldn't measure up." This comes from teens who are 100 percent sincere.

The danger in this kind of thinking is that it puts the emphasis on our *life* instead of *Christ's love*. Paul wrote, "What can separate us from the love of God?" (Rom. 8:34, 35).

Now if God loved us while we were sinners, does He love us less after we have begun trusting in His Son?

Let me illustrate. God has blessed my wife and me with four wonderful children: Terri, eleven years of age; Louis, nine; David, six; and Brad, three. Each one began walking at about ten months. Now do you think that they were in perfect control of themselves when the first step was taken? Of course not. What did I do when each one fell? Did I jerk them up and administer a severe spanking because they didn't succeed at first? How could I, when I was so thrilled at their *attempts* to walk that my shirt buttons were having trouble staying sewed on? Instead, I rushed to their side and said, "That's alright, get up and try it again."

And did they walk the second time they tried? Did you? Or even the third? Or fourth? Did my love for my children weaken because they failed to walk the first few times? Not at all. An earthly father's love is much stronger than that.

Now I ask you: Is it possible for an earthly father's love to be greater than that of the heavenly Father? Can a mere man be more understanding of his children and their weaknesses than our Lord who "needed not that any should testify of man; for he knew what was in man"?

"Get up and try it again" is Christ's way of dealing with those who have fallen. His death on the cross won't let us forget His love. He is the one to go to when you need another chance. And who

78

doesn't! There are times when with the poet we would say:

> I wish that there were some wonderful
> place
> Called the Land of Beginning again,
> Where all our mistakes and all our heart-
> aches
> And all of our poor selfish grief
> Could be dropped like a shabby old coat at
> the door,
> And never be put on again.

The "Land of Beginning Again" is where you now stand! Or it can be. Fresh beginnings — a new start — this is the message of this parable and the entire New Testament. The son who said, "No, sir," was allowed to change his mind! "If we confess our sins, he is faithful and just to forgive us our sins and to cleanse us from all unrighteousness" (I John 1:9). God has provided forgiveness of sins and power for overcoming for the same reason that erasers are put on pencils — He knows you will make some mistakes!

Which son in the parable did the will of the father? How could we miss the answer to that one! The second one takes home the honor because he saw his mistake and did something about it.

This parable makes the claim that God doesn't give up easily. However, a greater mistake could hardly be made than to think He will wait until a certain amount of wild oats is sown, or until it's more convenient. Those who plan to do the will of God "later" should beware. The Lord does *ask* to be invited in. But He only knocks on the door; He will not break it in. And whom do you know who has been given a written guarantee that the knocker will still be there tomorrow morning?

The teen who does the will of God knows that "a quitter never wins and a winner never quits." You *can* serve Christ! His forgiveness and power will keep you in spite of your weaknesses, *if you want to be kept!* He does not say "Follow me and do it yourself!" Rather, He says, "Follow me and *I* will make you. . . ." You turn over the new leaf; Christ will help you make it *stay* turned over!

EXPRESS YOUR OPINION

1. Why do you think the second son decided to change his mind and do the father's will?

2. Read about a young man named Demas in Colossians 4:14; Philemon 24; and II Timothy 4: 10 and discuss it in connection with the parable of the two sons.

3. Does this parable explain Jesus' attitude toward Peter when he denied Jesus?

4. Discuss some reasons why some say, No, and never change their minds.

5. Discuss some reasons why some say, Yes, and never change their minds.

PART THREE

RARE INVITATIONS

This is the Lord's doings; it is marvelous in our eyes.
—Psalm 118:23

When a Halo 9
Becomes a Noose

MATTHEW 12:43-45 (The New English Bible), THE UNOCCUPIED HOUSE

" 'WHEN AN UNCLEAN SPIRIT COMES out of a man it wanders over the deserts seeking a resting-place, and finds none. Then it says, "I will go back to the home I left." So it returns and finds the house unoccupied, swept clean, and tidy. Off it goes and collects seven other spirits more wicked than itself, and they all come in and settle down; and in the end the man's plight is worse than before. That is how it will be with this wicked generation.' "

ONE STUDENT, obviously hard pressed regarding a school assignment, wrote to *National Geographic*: "Would you get all the information you could possibly get and send it to me in the least time possible?" That student sounds about as frustrated as a teen-age girl locked in a room with a dozen new wigs and no mirror.

Fortunately, not every teen gets *that* frustrated! But that doesn't mean you haven't already experienced enough pressure, tension, and pain to side with a little girl, who after stumbling over a rock, said, "I wish all the world were cushioned."

Admittedly, frustrating experiences in your teens are bad enough, but the parable of the unoccupied house tells us there is something far worse. The frustrated life isn't as bad as an *empty* life. This parable gives the reason why a life can lose its vigor, purpose, and usefulness. It contains the secret of enjoying the Christian life. Teens who put this parable's lesson into practice find out why it *is* possible to become more excited about living for Christ than waiting for weekend dates and opening kick-offs.

The house in the parable is compared to a life. When we learn that the house was swept clean we get the picture of a life making a good start, like the first son in last chapter's parable.

But something happened. A life can be headed in the right direction and then change course. Maybe discouragement, defeat, or harsh criticism caused it. Or, maybe neglecting regular worship, daily devotions, and witnessing to others gradually made the Christian traveler wander off the "straight and narrow."

Shouting or Struggling

Now there are times when the Christian life slows down, and that's usually a dangerous period. Young Christians show clear-cut signs of growing up spiritually when they realize that this race can't always be run "full speed ahead." There's a point where every inch of progress is gained, not by shouting, but by struggling.

Those who try to ha, ha, ha their way through

often become so discouraged when faced with trials and temptations that they fold their hands. This period of discouragement is the time the house can become "unoccupied."

This is food for thought. A good life cannot stay that way just by eliminating the bad. It is possible to be more concerned about not being bad than being good! Concentrate on being of service and your life will maintain its meaning and worth. The following poem can be a plan for progress:

> Plan for more than you can do
> Then do it.
> Bite off more than you can chew
> Then chew it.
> Hitch your wagon to a star
> Keep your seat and there you are.

Emptiness and Usefulness

Our lives can become empty when we fear to face great responsibilities or hesitate too long to take advantage of opportunities. If we don't use our faith, we find out that "our doubts are traitors that make us lose the good we oft might win by fearing to attempt."

Accepting Christ is the great start toward living the greatest life, but like a bicycle, it has to be kept in motion or a spill is ahead. The challenge of discipleship calls for victorious living at home, on your dates, at your school, and wherever you go.

It can't be done? Don't believe it! Years ago, my eighth grade English teacher, Mrs. Christian, assigned the following poem to our class. All of us memorized "It Couldn't Be Done" by Edgar A. Guest. It has proved to be a great source of inspiration to me during frustrating times. Why don't you memorize it?

Somebody said that it couldn't be done,
  But he with a chuckle replied
That "maybe it couldn't" but he would be
      one
  Who wouldn't say so till he'd tried.
So he buckled right in with the trace of a
      grin
  On his face. If he worried he hid it.
He started to sing as he tackled the thing
  That couldn't be done, and he did it.

Somebody scoffed; "Oh, you'll never do
      that;
  At least no one has ever done it";
But he took off his coat and he took off his
      hat,
  And the first thing we knew he'd begun
      it.
With a lift of his chin and a bit of a grin,
  Without any doubting or quitting,
He started to sing as he tackled the thing
  That couldn't be done, and he did it.

There are thousands to tell you it cannot
      be done;
  There are thousands to prophesy fail-
      ure;
There are thousands to point out to you,
      one by one,
  The dangers that wait to assail you.
But just buckle in with a bit of a grin,
  Just take off your coat and go to it;
Just start to sing as you tackle the thing
  That "cannot be done," and you'll do
      it.

Anyway, not to go ahead for fear of failing
would be a mistake. Who would refuse to go fish-
ing for fear of not catching any fish? Who would

refuse to go shopping for fear of not being able to find what he wanted? Rather, try and fail than fail to try. A life without action invites trouble. Evil has sharp eyes and detects idleness. It also has friends who quickly join forces and move in, if given the chance. This might explain why one teen-ager in Oklahoma said that she felt pressured and confused, and wrote: "I hate the world and everything in it." A halo has to fall only a few inches to become a noose. So can your Christian life turn sour by dropping your activity output.

Keeping your life occupied with Christ will never allow evil a chance to take over. But this kind of life is no accident. Trust this to luck, time, or chance and you'll be about as sensible as the girl the following limerick tells about:

> She wore stockings inside out
> All through the summer heat;
> She said it cooled her off to turn
> The hose upon her feet!

A good starting place for guarding against a haunted house is your mind. "As a man thinketh in his heart, so is he." What you do and how you do it depend on how you *think*. Evil thoughts (the forerunner of evil actions) can't be kept out of your mind. They can be kept *in*, however. As Augustine said, "An evil thought passes through the door first as a stranger, then enters as a guest, then it installs itself as master."

However, minds filled with good thoughts leave little room for the bad. Here's inspired advice on "positive thinking":

> Whatsoever things are true
> Whatsoever things are honest

Whatsoever things are just
Whatsoever things are pure
Whatsoever things are lovely
Whatsoever things are of good report
. . . Think on these things.

And get set — you are ready to shift your life into overdrive! Keep your eye peeled for things you can do for others. Stay busy. Prodigals have more to do than return home. You can idle in neutral only so long, before you shift into *reverse*.

"The world steps aside for the man who knows where he's going." Make Colossians 3:23, "And whatsoever ye do, do it heartily, as to the Lord, and not unto men," your daily practice and your motion will always be forward!

EXPRESS YOUR OPINION

1. What part should your church program play in keeping your life from becoming unoccupied?

2. Discuss opportunities and responsibilities that teens have at home that contribute to the molding of character.

3. Find a verse in the four Gospels that tells us what kind of example of the active life of service Jesus was living.

4. Why do the biographies of great men and women stress what they *did*, rather than what they *did not* do?

5. Can you become too active? Explain.

"Why Can't 10
Miss Watson Fat Up?"

LUKE 11:5-10 (Phillips), THE NIGHT CALLER

"THEN HE ADDED:

"If any of you has a friend and goes to him in the middle of the night and says, 'Lend me three loaves, my dear fellow, for a friend of mine has just arrived after a journey and I have no food to put in front of him'; and then he answers from inside the house: 'Don't bother me with your troubles. The front door is locked and my children and I have gone to bed. I simply cannot get up now and give you anything!' Yet, I tell you, that even if he won't get up and give him what he wants simply because he is his friend, yet if he persists, he will rouse himself and give him everything he needs. And so I tell you, ask and it will be given you, search and you will find, knock and the door will be opened to you. The one who asks will always receive; the one who is searching will always find, and the door is opened to the man who knocks."

LUKE 18:1-8 (King James Version)

"AND HE SPAKE A PARABLE unto them to this end,

that men ought always to pray, and not to faint; Saying, There was in a city a judge, which feared not God, neither regarded man: And there was a widow in that city; and she came unto him saying, Avenge me of mine adversary. And he would not for a while; but afterward he said within himself, Though I fear not God, nor regard man; Yet because this widow troubleth me, I will avenge her, lest by her continual coming she weary me. And the Lord said, Hear what the unjust judge saith. And shall not God avenge his own elect, which cry day and night unto him, though he bear long with them? I tell you that he will avenge them speedily. Nevertheless, when the Son of man cometh, shall he find faith on the earth?"

REMEMBER IN *Huckleberry Finn* when Huck had a talk with Miss Watson about prayer? Later, he says:

"She told me to pray every day and whatever I asked for I would get it. But it wasn't so. I tried it.

"I set down one time back in the woods and had a long think about it. I said to myself, if a body can get anything they pray for why don't Deacon Winn get back the money he lost on pork? Why can't the widow get back her silver snuff-box that was stole? Why can't Miss Watson fat up?

"There's something in it when a body like the widow prays, but it don't work for me, and I reckon it don't work for only just the right kind."

Huck Finn wasn't the only one confused about prayer. Might we dare suggest that teens of today are more successful in talking parents into seeing the merits of allowance increases than in getting hoped-for answers to all their prayers? Could be. Complaints regarding unsuccessful prayers come thicker than tacklers at the one-foot line with last down and goal-to-go.

To teach us how to pray successfully, Jesus told two parables: the midnight caller, and the determined widow.

Take the first one. An emergency arises because an inconsiderate friend drops in at midnight. The custom in that day was to feed your guests before they went to bed, no matter what time they dropped in. Our poor host discovers that his cupboard is as bare as Mother Hubbard's.

So out into the night he goes to the nearest friendly neighbor. When he knocks on the door and tries to arouse his friend, he gets a response that we would expect. "Don't bother me, the door is locked by this time, and my children are in bed with me. I can't get up and give you anything."

When he hears this, does the desperate man throw up his hands and walk away muttering something about "my fair weather friends"? Why, no. He needs bread. His neighbor has some. It may be midnight but this is an emergency. He keeps on knocking. Jesus Himself told us what will happen: "I tell you . . . he will at last rise and give you whatever you want, *because you persist.*"

Fast Notions and Slow Motion

Here then is Jesus' point: Successful praying calls for an "I'll keep on, until you answer" attitude. A God who never sleeps is not going to be easily inconvenienced. He *stays* ready. But He wastes no time on those for whom prayer is not a highlight. His ear will never be caught by half-hearted bless me's punctuated with yawns.

> 'Tis not enough to bend the knee
>   And words of prayer to say;
> The heart must with the lips agree;
>   Or else we do not pray:
> For words, without the heart,
>   The Lord will never hear;
> Nor will He to those lips attend,
>   Whose prayers are not sincere.

Getting through to God takes effort: asking, seeking, knocking. And to those who will, He promised, "For *everyone* that asketh receiveth; and he that seeketh findeth; and to him that knocketh it shall be opened."

Sometimes the answer doesn't come as quickly as we think it should. It upsets us when God reacts to our emergencies in slow motion. But the answer will come. It may be, Yes. It might be, No. Sometimes it is, Wait. Of the three, Wait seems the hardest for us. Some can't wait very long and prayer seldom works for the impatient.

Friends give favors to each other, even in the middle of the night *if* determination is shown. But so will a calloused old judge who fears neither God nor man, if he's hounded long enough. A widow is the heroine in the second parable. Her first efforts to get the judge's help got the door slammed in her face. Before long, however, she got what she wanted. How? Not because the judge suddenly felt sorry for her, but because she made herself a nuisance to him.

Of course, Jesus wasn't comparing God to a stern, unfeeling judge. And that's just the point. If someone as hard-boiled as that would help her when she was in trouble, it is reasonable to expect a sharp-eyed, attentive heavenly Father to respond quickly to distress signals from needy saints.

The way some complain about unanswered prayer, you'd think God was cloud-chained and hard of hearing. Listening to them talk you get the idea that God is not greater than His responsibilities. They misunderstand that praying is not like rubbing Aladdin's lamp, that Jesus is not some kind of genie who makes our wishes His commands. Try asking Him to do your homework for you, if you don't believe it! He's our Lord, not our lackey; our Saviour, not our servant. Prayer under pressure loaded with determination is what it takes to get through to God!

We can feel free to go to Him. Feel free? We are *urged* to go to Him — and rest upon His promise to come to our aid. Don't wonder at the teens who are head over heels in love with Jesus! How can you feel sorry for youth who realize that they can depend upon Christ when the chips are down. He is well aware of your problems *and* their solutions. No one has ever been able to accuse Him of playing hookey from the here and now. "He is an ever present help in the time of trouble," and what follows is proof.

One night recently, my cousin, Cindy (not her real name), nineteen years old, and her steady, twenty-two, were held up by three hoods, one of whom held a gun at the back of Jerry's head. After getting their money, one of the hoods started for Cindy with intentions any teen is old enough to guess. Being a Christian, she knelt and began to pray. Suddenly the leader of the group spoke: "Oh, leave her alone. Let's get out of here." Since then Cindy understands better what David meant when he said: "I love the Lord, because he hath heard my voice and my supplications. . . . Therefore I will call upon him as long as I live" (Ps. 116:1, 2).

Here's the challenge the Lord hurled in this parable: "Try to outdo me at gift-giving!" And when you think of the gift of a breath-taking sunset, freedom, friendship, opportunity, the privilege of prayer, Calvary, and all the other gifts of life under God's rule, you can see that He'll not be outdone!

Has He given you any good gifts lately? "He that cometh to God must believe that he is, and that he is a rewarder of them that *diligently* seek him" (Heb. 11:6).

How diligently have *you* sought him?

EXPRESS YOUR OPINION

1. Does this parable teach us that prayer can be used much like a spare tire — only good in case of emergencies?

2. How would you explain the way to be friends with Jesus?

3. Discuss how Christ actually shows His love by saying, No, to some of our prayers.

4. Should prayer be used to get help on tests, confidence on the football field, or guidance in choosing dates? Why?

5. If you don't talk to Christ about the little things in your life, will your prayers in emergencies be as effective? Discuss.

You Can Be Wealthy **11**

LUKE 12:15-21 (The New English Bible), THE WEALTHY PAUPER

"Then he said to the people, 'Beware! Be on your guard against greed of every kind, for even when a man has more than enough, his wealth does not give him life.' And he told them this parable: 'There was a rich man whose land yielded heavy crops. He debated with himself: "What am I to do? I have not the space to store my produce. This is what I will do," said he: "I will pull down my storehouses and build them bigger. I will collect in them all my corn and other goods, and then say to myself, 'Man, you have plenty of good things laid by, enough for many years: take life easy, eat, drink, and enjoy yourself.'" But God said to him, "You fool, this very night you must surrender your life; you have made your money — who will get it now?" That is how it is with the man who amasses wealth for himself and remains a pauper in the sight of God.'"

HAVING JUST COME from an interview with the

guidance counselor, a high school student told his dad about his plans for the future. "I'm going to college, first," he said. "Next comes graduate school, and then specialized study."

Answered the father: "Did your guidance counselor happen – just happen – to suggest anything about a job eventually?"

A perfectly sensible question, don't you think? But that father, and others like him, might be relieved to know that, although today's teens spend more time in school, they also can expect to work more years and make more money than any generation of youth in our history.

The future looks promising, doesn't it – if you have dreams of dollars in your future, that is. But if your plans for prosperity leave no room for God in your life, you need a parable – the parable of the wealthy pauper. (Incidentally, money is not the only reason this parable is needed. Careers, associations – anything that threatens to take Christ from position number one in your life invites the lesson contained in this story.)

Back to the subject of money. Would it surprise you to know that Christ talked more about money and the wise use of possessions than anything else?

Why? Because money is the root of all evil? That's the way some have it, but that's not the way the Bible teaches it. "The *love* of money is the root of all evil" is the way Paul, the apostle, told it to a young man named Timothy. A proper understanding of the New Testament's stand regarding money teaches us that a lot of money will no more make us sinful than the lack of it will make us righteous. If we had our "druthers" we'd probably have to admit that:

One should not love money,
Of that I have no doubt.
    But I'm just as sure
    Being poor's no cure —
I'd rather be with than without!

This being true doesn't keep Christians from going off the deep end. Only Christ could give a man keen enough insight to write, "The world would be better off if people tried to become better, and people would become better if they would stop trying to become better off. But when everybody tries to become better, everybody is better off."

Christ knew that "striking it rich" makes too many get their nose too high in the air and feel that God is no longer necessary. Do you get this same idea from reading I Timothy 6:17-19? "Charge them that are rich in this world, that they be not highminded, nor trust in uncertain riches, but in the living God, who giveth us richly all things to enjoy; That they do good, that they be rich in good works, ready to distribute, willing to communicate; Laying up in store for themselves a good foundation against the time to come, that they may lay hold on eternal life."

Money and the Modern Mirage

The parable's title, the rich fool, is enough in itself to make eyes bulge and heads shake. Rich *fool?* Moderns scratch their heads at this and wonder, how can you be a fool if you're rich? And besides, if nothing is wrong with money, then why drag up a parable on the subject? Jesus must have meant it only for the money-mad citizens of His day!

But we know better. The senior editor of a leading magazine was right on the beam with this statement: "In our society, money is worshiped as the root of all happiness; it is more godlike than God."

Has this polluted idea seeped into teen-age minds? Ask your classmates what their idea of success is, and you'll have your answer quicker than you can respond to a fire drill signal. Is preparing for a lifetime of service the popular trend in your school? Or are we coming closer to the truth if we suggest that what drives most of the ambitious are dreams of swollen safety accounts, luxurious living, and a life free from stress and strain?

Can anyone look closely at the rich man in the parable without seeing a painful reflection of himself? Not that the fellow was bad. Evidently, he had gotten his wealth honestly. He was a hard worker who had devoted all his attention to his work.

And that was just the trouble. He had given *all* his attention, thought, and time to his work. He had left God completely out of the picture. It's easy to see why, too, when you count the number of references he makes to himself — twelve in three verses! There's no room for God in a life filled with self.

Reading further we begin to feel pity for him when he says, "And I will say to my soul, Soul, thou hast much goods laid up for many years; Take thine ease, eat, drink and be merry." The life of Riley lay ahead — or so he thought.

"But [Who can read this interruption and keep from trembling?] God said unto him, Thou fool, this night thy soul shall be required of thee; Then whose shall these things be which thou hast provided?" The God whom the rich man neglected interrupts these "best laid plans." His barns are running over, but his soul is bankrupt. And now he must give an account! Add to that the thought of all that he had worked for going into the hands of others and then ask yourself if that's the kind of success you want. "So is he that layeth up treasure for himself, and is not rich toward God."

Christ wants no one to get the wrong idea as to life's meaning. "Take heed . . ." He says, "for a man's life consisteth not in the abundance of the things which he possesseth." You can be wealthy if you're "rich toward God." Your Sunday best may be hand-me-downs, but if Christ is your daily friend and guide, you're rich beyond compare. For money can't buy peace of mind, forgiveness of sins, fellowship with Jesus, and hope beyond this life! Go ahead and prepare and work — even prosper if you can, so long as Christ is first in your life. But never forget this: "For what shall it profit a man if he gain the whole world and lose his soul?" (Matt. 16:26).

EXPRESS YOUR OPINION

1. A rich young ruler once had a talk with Jesus. Read about it in Matthew 19:16-26 and discuss how it relates to this parable.

2. If you live a good enough life will God prosper you materially?

3. Why do we admire those Christians who put the will of God before anything else?

4. Do you have to be rich to feel that you don't need God?

5. Name as many things as you can that are more important than money.

For a Pain in the Neck **12**

MATTHEW 18:21-35 (King James Version), THE UNMERCIFUL SERVANT

"THEN CAME PETER TO HIM, and said, Lord, how oft shall my brother sin against me, and I forgive him? till seven times? Jesus saith unto him, I say not unto thee, Until seven times: but, Until seventy times seven.

"Therefore is the kingdom of heaven likened unto a certain king, which would take account of his servants. And when he had begun to reckon, one was brought unto him which owed him ten thousand talents. But forasmuch as he had not to pay, his lord commanded him to be sold, and his wife, and children, and all that he had, and payment to be made. The servant therefore fell down, and worshipped him, saying, Lord, have patience with me, and I will pay thee all. Then the lord of that servant was moved with compassion, and loosed him, and forgave him the debt.

"But the same servant went out, and found one of his fellowservants, which owed him an hundred pence: and he laid hands on him, and took him by the throat, saying, Pay me that thou owest. And his fellowservant fell down at his feet, and besought him, saying, Have patience with me, and I will pay thee all. And he would not: but went and cast him into prison, till he should pay the debt. So when his fellowservants saw what was done, they were very sorry, and came and told unto their lord all that was done.

"Then his lord, after that he had called him, said unto him, O thou wicked servant, I forgave thee all that debt, because thou desiredst me: Shouldest not thou also have had compassion on thy fellowservant, even as I had pity on thee? And his lord was wroth and delivered him to the tormentors, till he should pay all that was due unto him.

"So likewise shall my heavenly Father do also unto you, if ye from your hearts forgive not every one his brother their trespasses."

WHAT WOULD HAPPEN if an irresistible force were to meet an immovable object?

This famous question was once asked a football player in a physics class. He said, "If an irresistible force struck an immovable object, I guess they would just stand there and *strain*."

He might have been describing something else, too: What happens when two people try to overcome each other's opposition by using "an eye for an eye" technique. Nobody ever wins in this kind of battle. They both "just stand there and strain." This parable shows us how to keep from having to "stand there and strain" when we're rubbed the wrong way.

Actions and Reactions

Someone must've rubbed Peter the wrong way

— more than once — because he asked Jesus, "How oft shall my brother sin against me, and I forgive him? Till seven times?" A touch of acid is added to this question with "my brother." Christians are not supposed to sin against each other, but they sometimes do. Like Peter, we, too, wonder when wronged, just how much of this should I take?

Jesus' answer must've caused Peter to feel like a teen who takes home a test paper with a grade of ninety-three only to have Dad say, "Why didn't you make a hundred?" Peter's ears must've burned when Jesus said that he must forgive "seventy times seven."

Instead of showing impatience or disgust with His outspoken disciple, Jesus proceeded to use Peter's question to teach the world the parable of the unforgiving servant.

A certain servant owed his king ten thousand talents, or about ???????? dollars. He was asked to pay up. He pulled his pockets inside out — nothing. The king demanded payment, which meant that the servant, his family, and all that he owned would have to be sold.

"The servant therefore fell down, and worshipped him, saying, Lord, have patience with me, and I will pay thee all. Then the lord of that servant was moved with compassion, and loosed him, and forgave him the debt."

Pardoned! The poor wretch had touched the king's heart. Because of the king's mercy, the servant was off the hook, scot free.

. . . And there you are, too, if you're a Christian. For this is your life's story. Your name is written in the Lamb's book of life, and what did you do to deserve it? What a terrible condition sinful man must have been in to make Calvary necessary!

We who are so freely forgiven ought to find it easier to forgive.

But not so in our parable. (And you can already sense the dramatic climax this parable is leading to.) "But the same servant went out, and found one of his fellow servants which owed him a hundred pence" (about ?? dollars).

Well, now the fellow has a chance to show mercy himself. But no. "He laid hands on him and took him by the throat saying, Pay me what thou owest. And his fellow servant fell down at his feet and besought him saying, Have patience with me and I will pay thee all [the same plea he himself had given a short while ago]. And he would not: but went and cast him into prison, till he should pay the debt."

"Whatever You Sow . . ."

As soon as word of this reached the king, the unforgiving servant was found and brought before him. The enraged king thundered: "I forgave thee all the debt, because thou desiredst me; shouldest not thou also have had compassion on thy fellow servant, even as I had pity on thee?" His wrong had boomeranged. Galatians 6:7 had caught up with him. He was thrown into prison where he would stay until his debt was paid — which really meant a life sentence.

By this time sweat must have broken out on Peter's face. But he wasn't prepared for the final stroke. "So also my heavenly Father will do to *everyone* of you, if you from your hearts forgive not everyone his brother their trespasses."

Forgiveness, this parable teaches, cannot be limited to that which God gives man. It must then

104

be extended from man to man, "from the heart!" A vertical forgiveness must become horizontal.

Grudge-holders pay a big price. So do the envious and jealous. The human body rebels when emotions are stirred by these reactions. Medical science has discovered that hate can actually cause "a pain in the neck." Headaches, upset stomachs, ulcers — these are just a few of the ways we can suffer when we refuse to learn this parable's lesson.

If you've ever had to apologize, you know how tough it is. But it can be even tougher when you *forgive* — for the *right* reason.

> If I forgive an injury
> Because resenting would poison *me* —
> I may feel noble, I may feel splendid,
> But it isn't exactly what Christ intended.

Christian teens are to "be . . . kind to one another, tenderhearted, forgiving one another, even as God for Christ's sake hath forgiven you" (Eph. 4:32).

Forgiveness and Forgetfulness

Did you ever hear of Fred Merkle? If not, your dad probably has, especially if he is a baseball fan. For on an afternoon in 1908, Merkle, then only nineteen, pulled the most historic boner in the history of baseball.

Playing his first game as a nineteen-year-old for the New York Giants against the Chicago Cubs, Merkle missed second base on a crucial play. The Cubs protested and even though the Giants won, the game had to be replayed. This time the Cubs won. Fred Merkle's boner not only cost the Giants the game but the championship that year.

More than fifty-five years have passed since that day. A lot of things have come and gone, but do you think people have forgotten what Fred Merkle did?

He was asked that question several summers ago. He said that when he is with a group of people and gets up to leave, someone never fails to shout after him: "So long, Fred. Don't forget to touch second base."

A strange thing about some people is that they can remember a mistake ten times — no, a thousand times — longer than a good deed. Thank God, that's one of the greatest differences between God and man. God can't remember sins that have been repented of. "Their sins and their iniquities will I remember no more" (Heb. 8:12).

God forgives and forgets. Match that for changing lives and chasing away the blues! But we are to imitate Him. Emerson said of Lincoln, "His heart was as great as the world, but there was no room in it to hold the memory of a wrong."

Next time in praying the Lord's Prayer, you say, "Forgive us our trespasses as we forgive those who trespass against us" remember this parable's point: forgiveness must be given if it is to be gotten.

A teen-ager who can forgive those who have sinned against him, not because failing to do so "would drag me to his level" or "because I feel it my duty," but because "my Lord has forgiven me" rates an A+ in meeting an obligation of love. And besides, being able to "overcome evil with good" pulls you closer to maturity than shaving twice a day or having worn high heels "ever since I can remember." Christ can give you a testimony like this:

He drew a circle that shut me out
Heretic, rebel, a thing to flout.
But love and I had the wit to win:
We drew a circle that took him in!

EXPRESS YOUR OPINION

1. Read Luke 23:33, 34, and discuss it in connection with the parable.

2. What's wrong with the following reasons for forgiving others: "Oh, well, I'll just consider the source." "Of course, I can be big about this." "My influence may suffer if I don't give in."

3. Is it harder to forgive than to ask to be forgiven? Discuss.

4. Can a person who has a hard time thinking of anything he's done wrong be as forgiving as Christ taught? Explain.

5. Why must a person have a deep awareness of what Jesus' death on the cross means to him before he can sincerely forgive others?

PART FOUR

NOBLE OBLIGATIONS

*It is to God alone that we have to answer
for our actions.*
—Romans 14:12 (Phillips)

Take the Bat
Off Your Shoulder **13**

LUKE 19:11-27 (King James Version), **THE TEN POUNDS**

"And as they heard these things, he added and spake a parable, because he was nigh to Jerusalem, and because they thought that the kingdom of God should immediately appear. He said therefore, A certain nobleman went into a far country to receive for himself a kingdom, and to return. And he called his ten servants, and delivered them ten pounds, and said unto them, Occupy till I come.

"But his citizens hated him, and sent a message after him, saying, We will not have this man to reign over us. And it came to pass, that when he was returned, having received the kingdom, then he commanded these servants to be called unto him, to whom he had given the money, that he might know how much every man had gained by trading. Then came the first, saying, Lord, thy pound hath gained ten pounds. And he said unto him, Well, thou good servant: because thou hast been faithful in a very little, have thou authority over ten cities. And the second, came, saying, Lord, thy pound hath gained five pounds. And he

111

said likewise to him, Be thou also over five cities.

"And another came, saying, Lord, behold here is thy pound, which I have kept laid up in a napkin: for I feared thee, because thou art an austere man: thou takest up that thou layedst not down, and reapest that thou didst not sow. And he saith unto him, Out of thine own mouth will I judge thee, thou wicked servant. Thou knewest that I was an austere man, taking up that I laid not down, and reaping that I did not sow: wherefore then gavest not thou my money into the bank, that at my coming I might have required mine own with usury?

"And he said unto them that stood by, Take from him the pound, and give it to him that hath ten pounds. (And they said unto him, Lord, he hath ten pounds.) For I say unto you, That every one which hath shall be given; and from him that hath not, even that he hath shall be taken away from him. But those mine enemies, which would not that I should reign over them, bring hither, and slay them before me."

WAS ANYONE EVER MISUNDERSTOOD more than Jesus Christ? And yet how patient was the Master with those who lacked understanding. Some of his greatest recorded lessons were given for "slow learners." Freshmen in the faith have a lot to learn, and Jesus has never been known to become impatient and aggravated in dealing with sincere seekers of the truth.

The parable of the pounds is a perfect example. It was an answer aimed at correcting the mistaken idea on the part of His followers (keep in mind that teen-agers were surely among them) "that the kingdom of heaven was to appear immediately."

Jesus was so extraordinary that such a miracle was possible. Even the teens in the crowd that day knew that anyone who could raise the dead, open blind eyes, unstop deaf ears, straighten crooked limbs, and heal broken hearts by the power of His word was capable of world leadership! It won't be long now, they must've thought. From Jerusalem, Jesus will loose His mighty power over all mankind. Then the wars will stop, disease and suffering will disappear. We will have heaven on earth. The kingdom of God will have come.

But they were wrong. The "whiz kids" must have known it, as soon as Jesus gave the secret away by beginning the story with, "A nobleman went into a far country. . . ." "So that's the way it's going to be!" they must have thought. And their dreams, like Humpty Dumpty, must have had a great fall.

Their interest in the story was suddenly heightened, however, as Jesus continued by telling them of the parting conversation this nobleman had with ten of his servants. He gave them ten pounds and said, "Trade with these till I come."

The lesson becomes clearer. Not only will Jesus' followers have to wait for Him to return, they are expected to *work*. While He is away, He wants His disciples to be busy looking after His interests. This means being responsible for what is done when opportunity presents itself.

This tosses the lesson into our laps, too, doesn't it? Jesus still has not returned. When will He? "Where is the promise of His coming?" We should be looking — as we are laboring.

No wonder then that Christian teens can be

called opportunists! The only youth in the world with a worthwhile reason for alertness, aggressiveness and preparedness are those servants of Jesus Christ, who realize they have a task to perform, a service to render. They have a reason for being, because they are being for something — the cause of Christ in the world today. For them, what one is *achieving* matters more than what one is *enjoying*. Purpose instead of pleasure occupies most of their thinking. The result? They enjoy a higher, richer, and more exciting life than other youth do in their wildest dreams!

But what will happen to those who missed their opportunities and shirked their responsibilities? Jesus gave an answer to that one, too. One day the nobleman returned. The servants who worked with what they had been given were awarded with positions of great authority and prestige. However, one of the ten had betrayed the Master's trust. He had done nothing with his opportunities and advantages during the nobleman's absence. "Don't do today what you can put off until tomorrow" was his philosophy. And so daily he met and missed his opportunities. He was like the writer of the following poem:

> Procrastination is my sin,
> It causes me endless sorrow.
> But I've made up my mind to quit,
> And I will begin — tomorrow.

In ancient Greece, there is a stone tablet on which a peculiar-looking statue once stood. Carved on the tablet is this dialogue:

"What is thy name, O statue?"
"My name is opportunity."
"Why art thou standing on tiptoe?"

114

"So I can be ever alert and ready to go out and meet men as they walk daily through life."

"And why is thy hair brushed down in long strands across thy forehead?"

"So men can easily seize me as they meet me."

"Why is the back of thy head so bald?"

"So men may know that once I have passed, I cannot be caught."

Nobody knows how helpless you feel when an opportunity is missed as do baseball players at bat. "Fellows," my coach used to say, "I don't want you to strike out, but if you do, go down swinging. Don't stand there and take a third strike with the bat on your shoulder." When the ball's in the catcher's mitt, it's too late. The opportunity's gone.

You can't do much about the opportunities you've missed in the past, but you *can* take advantage of opportunities you will have today, and from now on. A Spirit-filled life with "affections set on things above" can successfully meet the challenge.

And if you do "strike out" occasionally, go down swinging! Remember: if you can get a hit in only one out of three attempts, you can make any major league team in the world! But to get a hit, you've got to take the bat off your shoulder.

You aren't expected to be able to do it all. Just make sure you're doing what you can. You can be bigger than your responsibilities if you know that responsibility means your response to God's ability!

EXPRESS YOUR OPINION

1. Compare Acts 1:9-14 with the lesson taught on the parable of the pounds. Discuss.

2. Is it possible to apply the lesson taught in the parable of the talents and not apply the lesson taught in the parable of the pounds? Explain.

3. Why doesn't this parable talk about luck?

4. How should this parable influence your attitude toward your schoolwork?

5. Discuss daily opportunities to glorify God that come to us all, but are usually overlooked.

Be a V.I.P. 14

"AND HE PUT FORTH A PARABLE to those which were
bidden, when he marked how they chose out the
chief rooms; saying unto them, When thou art
bidden of any man to a wedding, sit not down in
the highest room; lest a more honorable man than
thou be bidden of him; And he that bade thee and
him come and say to thee, Give this man place;
and thou begin with shame to take the lowest room.
But when thou art bidden, go and sit down in the
lowest room; that when he that bade thee cometh,
he may say unto thee, Friend, go up higher: then
shalt thou have worship in the presence of them
that sit at meat with thee. For whosoever exalteth
himself shall be abased; and he that humbleth himself shall be exalted."

A YOUNG LADY in her teens was filling out an application for college. She came to the question,
"Are you a leader?" She had never been a leader
so she answered, No, even though she was afraid

117

it might disqualify her for admission. In the reply from one of the college officials came this surprising message: "A study of the application blanks reveals that this year our college will have 1,452 leaders. Therefore, we are accepting you because we feel it imperative that they have one follower."

That teen might not have known it, but if everybody were like her, Jesus wouldn't have found it necessary to tell us the parable of the status seeker.

Status means rank or position and is sought after by everyone who wants to be "somebody." This desire of recognition and appreciation may be stronger than the desire to be loved; maybe even stronger than the desire of self-preservation!

In this parable Jesus cautions us against "thinking more highly of ourselves, than we ought." Those having a tendency to "put on the dog" will thank Him for this reminder of what will eventually happen if this way of behaving is not halted.

The fellow in the parable was "put down" because he wanted to be a V.I.P. (a very important person). He wanted up front where everybody could see him — the way he prayed, sang, the clothes he wore. He's the type who, if he were asked "are you humble?" would reply, "I certainly am humble, and proud of it, too!"

Rushing for prominent places in church is just one way to feed the hunger for self-importance. Others are:

The fake-front technique. Some have deep feelings of weakness. Wishing to hide these feelings from others they will "cover up" by dressing in "way out" fashions, or they will be constantly letting off "self-esteem," or they will call attention to themselves by talking and laughing too loudly. All these methods act as a smoke screen to hide from others what they are ashamed — or afraid — of revealing.

The sour-grapes attitude. This one comes from the famous writing of Aesop, a Greek slave, who lived before Christ was born. Aesop told of a fox seeing a delicious-looking cluster of grapes hanging from a tree. After trying in vain to jump high enough to reach the grapes, the fox walked away saying to himself, "Oh, well, they were probably sour anyway." Those having a "sour-grape" attitude belittle what they would like to have, but can't. Examples are good grades, success in sports, membership in certain social groups, and the like.

The daydream escape. To accomplish their desires in this real world is impossible. So they create in their mind a world that offers all that this world has denied them. Often these daydreams are fed by fairy tale fiction and similar types of literature. Many retreat into a "make-believe" world to satisfy ambition and thus enjoy a cheaply gained feeling of importance.

Blame the other fellow. This attitude shows up in remarks such as, "My teacher flunked me because he didn't like me," or "No, I don't attend church because too many two-faced Christians are going there."

Chip-on-the-shoulder sensitivity. When frustrated, some get their feelings hurt at the slightest remark. They must be handled with "kid gloves." They act like a baby when they're not treated like a grownup. Someone once said, "A chip on the shoulder is a sign there's wood higher up"!

Dirt throwing technique. Some cannot bear to see others succeed, because this makes them feel cheated of opportunity and honor. To regain a feeling of self-importance in this instance is easy:

Pull oneself up by pulling the other person down by criticism. Jealousy and criticism are twins which always go together. But remember, "He who throws dirt is losing ground."

Recognition by Substitution

Did you detect a serious weakness in the above ways of achieving a feeling of self-importance and recognition? In every case this feeling (which we all must have) came as the result of substituting self-flattery and deceit for the wholesome ways of gaining appreciation.

This kind of pride makes prisoners of those who have it. In one of the classic books in American social science, the writer notes, "In order to gain and to hold the esteem of men it is not sufficient merely to possess wealth and power. The wealth must be in evidence, for esteem is awarded only in evidence."

Hollywood can furnish all the proof of this we need. One rock-and-roll star collects cars the way some collect stamps; he has fourteen. An actress who is known for her tape measure talent has a house with forty rooms, seven bedrooms, and thirteen bathrooms. A comedian spends more money on buttons than many men spend on suits; he pays $60 per suit for his golden darlings!

Merril B. Friend, a Hollywood psychiatrist said, "Many movie stars are like kids at Christmas who want the biggest trucks, and the most complicated toys, so other kids will come to their homes to play with them."

Royal Recognition

Does all this suggest that Christian youth ought

to have no pride? Not at all. Christian teens have much in which to glory. But unlike those who reject Christ, they are *elevated* not degraded by the object of their pride. The crowd's opinion, taste, moral standards, and activities does not dictate their actions and its threat to withdraw its approval and acceptance fails to overpower them.

Why? Their approval and acceptance come from God! Their names have been written in "Heaven's Who's Who," the Lamb's book of life! Those who know their approval comes from God and who work to please only Him will find themselves in a very unusual position. They are set free from that miserable type of life which is tormented by abnormal concern for the approval of people. It should be enough to know your plans, activities, and achievements get "heavenly attention." Once this attitude is developed, people's recognition will not make you puff up, and the lack of it will not make you give up. The only true V.I.P.'s are Christians who are personally acquainted with Jesus Christ. "Thus saith the Lord . . . let him that glorieth, glory in this, that he understandeth and knoweth me."

EXPRESS YOUR OPINION

1. Does Christ want us to have a poor attitude toward ourselves?

2. Discuss the ways in which sinful pride might show itself in participating in the church program.

3. Would having no pride at all be desirable? Discuss.

4. Humility is a Christlike virtue. How can you possess it? (The following poem may help.)

INDISPENSABLE?

Sometimes, when you're feeling important,
  Sometimes, when your ego's in bloom,
Sometimes, when you take it for granted
  You're the best qualified in the room;

Sometimes, when you feel that your going
  Would leave an unfillable hole,
Just follow this simple instruction
  And see how it humbles your soul:

Take a bucket and fill it with water,
  Put your hand in it, up to your wrist;
Pull it out — and the hole that's remaining
  Is the measure of how you'll be missed.

5. Explain how humility, godly pride, ambition and persistency can work together in the Christian's daily life.

Use Your Head **15**

LUKE 16:1-9 (Phillips), THE SHREWD SCOUNDREL

"THEN THERE IS THIS STORY he told his disciples:

"'Once there was a rich man whose agent was reported to him to be mismanaging his property. So he summoned him and said: "What's this that I hear about you? Give me an account of your stewardship — you're not fit to manage my household any longer." At this the agent said to himself: "What am I going to do now that my employer is taking away the stewardship from me? I am not strong enough to dig and I can't sink to begging. Ah, I know what I'll do so that when I lose my position people will welcome me into their homes!" So he sent for each one of his master's debtors. "How much do you owe my master?" he said to the first. "A hundred barrels of oil," he replied. "Here," replied the agent, "take your bill, sit down, hurry up and write in fifty." Then he said to another, "And what's the size of your debt?" "A thousand bushels of wheat," he replied. "Take your bill," said the agent, "and write in eight hundred." Now the master praised this rascally steward because he had been so careful for his own future. For the children of this world are considerably more shrewd in dealing with their contemporaries then the children of light. Now my advice to you is to use "money," tainted as it is, to make yourselves friends, so that when it comes to an end they may welcome you into eternal habitations.'"

WHAT'S THIS? Does this parable catch Jesus in a weak moment? Those who are habitual cookers of instant "I told you so's" are headed for red-faced surprise, if they miss the point of this bold story.

Jesus has not let down the honesty standard. Neither is he recommending that we practice the dishonest manager's morals. What Christ *is* bragging on, is the wise way the fellow used his head in an emergency.

And how about this guy! His sins and his boss had found him out. He'd had it. What to do? His solution classifies him as ingenious and qualifies him for top position in any "advanced-standing course." He quickly calls for the men who owe his master. He reduces their bills and makes lifetime friends out of them. As long as they live, they will remember his generosity. This is as he had planned, for who knows? Being out of a job, he just might have to sample their generosity!

In short, Jesus likes the way the man *thinks*, not the way he acts. And this *is* news to some! For the idea some have is that ignorance is prerequisite for becoming a Christian. Teens who use their heads appeal to Christ. He appreciates intelligence.

In taking an exam, a student came to this question: How would you determine the height of a building, using an ameroid barometer?

What the student lacked in technical knowledge, he made up in common sense. This is what he said: "I would lower the barometer on a string and measure the string." Now *that's* the kind of thinking through things that Christ likes to see!

Christian teens can — and should — become "wise as serpents." Quick thinkers are needed in these hectic days when emergencies are the order of the day. But the demand is greater than the supply. During your "green years" you ought to be dreaming, but don't neglect exercising your mind other ways, too. As a California professor wrote:

> Can one think and not wonder?
> I wonder.
> Can one wonder and not think?
> I wonder.
> But the wonder is to think.
> I think.

One of the great mistakes young Christians can make is that of thinking "Now that I'm a Christian I'll leave everything to Christ; He'll take good care of my responsibilities." You can be "dry behind the ears" and still be taken in by this. During the Reformation, an extreme sect called the Abecedarians, refused all human instruction. They wouldn't even learn to read or write, thinking the Holy Spirit would teach them all they needed to know (no homework or tests for them!). So they were named for the ABC's they refused to learn.

Now don't get the wrong idea. We are to be dependent upon God; we are to rely upon the Holy Spirit for help. But if you think that Christ will do your work for you, try asking Him to take

125

your final exams! We are expecting the impossible if we believe that God gave us a mind and will do our thinking for us, too!

Thinking is hard work and takes effort. But a great man isn't afraid of it. In your history books you read about Alexander Hamilton who was praised for his brilliance. He wrote: "Men give me credit for some genius. All the genius I have lies in this: When I have a subject in hand, I study it profoundly. Day and night it is before me. My mind becomes persuaded with it. Then the effort which I have made is what people are pleased to call the fruit of genius. It is the fruit of labor and thought."

Think of what would happen to our families, churches, schools, and cities if teens took to this kind of diligent study of the Bible, Christian literature and their subjects at school!

Christians "twix twelve and twenty" need not blush if they feel like Woodrow Wilson who said, "I use not only all the brains I have, but all I can borrow." Being a successful Christian amounts to more than "feeling great" during song service or at camp retreats. If, like Paul, you "know whom I have believed" you will realize the need to "*study* to show yourself approved unto God. . . ."

Those who neglect their studies find themselves in Jack's shoes:

Jack: "What should I do with my weekend?"

Friend: "Put a hat over it!"

Some time ago one of the Nashville, Tennessee, papers, *The Nashville Banner,* carried the story of a teen-ager named Roger Betenbaugh of South Carolina. Roger was riding in a car with three of his friends when the driver started taking foolish chances. Roger told them to let him out. They tried to get him to "be a good sport" and go along with the crowd.

But to Roger reckless driving was idiotic. This was an emergency. He knew what would happen, so he insisted they stop the car. Little did he realize when they sped off that he would never see his three buddies again. For a few minutes later all three were killed in an accident.

Christian young people need a lot of wisdom to know how to conduct themselves properly in today's complicated world. Is this kind of wisdom available? You can read the answer to that one in the book of James. "If any of you lack wisdom, let him ask of God, that giveth to all men liberally. . . . But let him ask in faith, nothing wavering . . ." (James 1:5, 6).

EXPRESS YOUR OPINION

1. Are Christian teens to be classified as good thinkers? Why?

2. Is it possible to be a Christian and still not use your head? Discuss using your head in selecting and accepting dates, in planning your future, and in choosing your close friends.

3. A wise man once said, "Keep your friendship in good repair." Apply that to this parable.

4. Compare the parable of the good Samaritan with the parable of the shrewd scoundrel.

5. Should a Christian teen be popular if he practices what is taught in this chapter's parable? Why?

DATE DUE